Python

P H R A S E B O O K

ESSENTIAL CODE AND COMMANDS

Brad Dayley

DEVELOPER'S LIBRARY

Sams Publishing, 800 East 96th Street, Indianapolis, Indiana 46240 USA

Trademarks

All terms mentioned in this book that are known to be trademarks or service marks have been appropriately capitalized. Sams Publishing cannot attest to the accuracy of this information. Use of a term in this book should not be regarded as affecting the validity of any trademark or service mark.

Warning and Disclaimer

Every effort has been made to make this book as complete and as accurate as possible, but no warranty or fitness is implied. The information provided is on an "as is" basis. The author and the publisher shall have neither liability nor responsibility to any person or entity with respect to any loss or damages arising from the information contained in this book.

Bulk Sales

Sams Publishing offers excellent discounts on this book when ordered in quantity for bulk purchases or special sales. For more information, please contact

> **U.S. Corporate and Government Sales**
> **1-800-382-3419**
> **corpsales@pearsontechgroup.com**

For sales outside the United States, please contact

> **International Sales**
> **international@pearsoned.com**

The Safari® Enabled icon on the cover of your favorite technology book means the book is available through Safari Bookshelf. When you buy this book, you get free access to the online edition for 45 days. Safari Bookshelf is an electronic reference library that lets you easily search thousands of technical books, find code samples, download chapters, and access technical information whenever and wherever you need it.

To gain 45-day Safari Enabled access to this book:

- Go to http://www.samspublishing.com/safarienabled
- Complete the brief registration form
- Enter the coupon code IZIK-GNBH-NGLQ-42HB-LZPB

If you have difficulty registering on Safari Bookshelf or accessing the online edition, please e-mail customer-service@safaribooksonline.com.

Acquisitions Editors Jenny Watson Mark Taber	**Managing Editor** Patrick Kanouse	**Indexer** Heather McNeil	**Publishing Coordinator** Vanessa Evans
Development Editor Songlin Qiu	**Project Editor** Tonya Simpson	**Proofreader** Mike Henry	**Book Designer** Gary Adair
	Copy Editor Sarah Kearns	**Technical Editor** Tim Boronczyk	**Page Layout** TnT Design, Inc.

Table of Contents

About the Author

Brad Dayley is a senior software engineer in Novell's
Nterprise Development Group. He has 14 years of
experience installing, troubleshooting, and developing
Novell's products for NetWare and Linux. He is the
co-author of *Novell's Guide to Resolving Critical Server
Issues*, as well as seven other Novell Press titles on the
ZENworks suite.

When he is not writing books or software, he can be
found biking, hiking, and/or Jeeping somewhere in the
remote regions of the Pacific Northwest with his wife,
DaNae, and four sons.

Dedication

For D,
A & F!

Acknowledgments

My sincere gratitude goes out to the following persons, without whom this book could not have happened:

To my wife, who provides all the inspiration and drive behind everything I do, words cannot say enough.

To my friends at Novell, especially Christine Williams, who force me to be more intelligent and creative than I would necessarily like to be, thanks for your support and friendship.

To my editors, who made the book readable, checked on my technical accuracy, and kept me on track, you all are great (and picky). It seems that nothing gets by you. To Jenny Watson, thanks for being such a great editor over the years and getting this book rolling, I wish you the best of luck. Thanks to Mark Taber for handling a tough transition and keeping the book on track; you've kept me going and helped make this book fun to write. To Songlin Qiu, Damon Jordan, and especially Timothy Boronczyk, thank you for helping me convert my thoughts and ramblings into a clean, coherent and technically accurate manuscript.

We Want to Hear from You!

As the reader of this book, *you* are our most important critic and commentator. We value your opinion and want to know what we're doing right, what we could do better, what areas you'd like to see us publish in, and any other words of wisdom you're willing to pass our way.

You can email or write me directly to let me know what you did or didn't like about this book—as well as what we can do to make our books stronger.

Please note that I cannot help you with technical problems related to the topic of this book, and that due to the high volume of mail I receive, I might not be able to reply to every message.

When you write, please be sure to include this book's title and author as well as your name and phone or email address. I will carefully review your comments and share them with the author and editors who worked on the book.

Email: opensource@samspublishing.com

Mail: Mark Taber
            Associate Publisher
            Sams Publishing
            800 East 96th Street
            Indianapolis, IN 46240 USA

Reader Services

Visit our website and register this book at www.samspublishing.com/register for convenient access to any updates, downloads, or errata that might be available for this book.

Introduction

I was excited when my editor asked me to write a phrasebook on the Python language. The phrasebook is one of the smallest books I have ever written; however, it was one of the hardest.

The idea of a conventional phrasebook is to provide readers with quick phrases that actually mean something in the language. The Python phrasebook is designed to provide you with meaningful Python phrases that you can actually understand and use to quickly begin programming Python applications.

The content of this book is based on Python 2.4. You should keep in mind that the Python language is constantly being added to. I would recommend visiting the Python website at http://www.python.org to familiarize yourself with accessing the online documentation, available extensions, and any changes that are occurring.

This book is not a reference manual or language guide that encompasses the entire language—that's not the purpose. The purpose is to provide you with a small, simple-to-use phrasebook that will get you going and provide a quick, easy reference later as you delve into new areas of the language.

When designing the content for this book, I tried to come up with the most relevant and interesting phrases that will actually help programs accomplish tasks that are pertinent to real-world needs. I welcome your comments and any phrases that you feel really need to be added to this book.

NOTE: Almost all the sample code used in this book is taken from actual working files. For your convenience, the Python scripts, CGI scripts, and HTML and XML documents that are shown as examples in the phrases of this book are available for download from the publisher's website. Register your book at www.samspublishing.com/register and download the code examples from this book. Feel free to modify them for your own needs.

I hope that you enjoy the phrases in this book and that they will be useful to you.

Understanding Python

Python is an extremely powerful and dynamic object-oriented programming language. It has similarities to scripting languages such as Perl, Scheme, and TCL, as well as other languages such as Java and C.

This chapter is designed to give you a quick glimpse into the Python language to help you understand the phrases in the subsequent chapters. It is not meant to be comprehensive; however, it should give you a feel for the language and help you understand the basics so that you can refer to the Python documentation for more information.

Why Use Python?

There are several reasons to use Python. It is one of the easier languages to pick up and start using, and yet it can be extremely powerful for larger applications. The following are just some of the good points of Python:

- **Portability**—Python runs on almost every operating system, including Linux/UNIX, Windows, Mac, OS 2, and others.

- **Integration**—Python can integrate with COM, .NET, and CORBA objects. There is a Jython implementation to allow the use of Python on any Java platform. IronPython is an implementation that gives Python programmers access to the .NET libraries. Python can also contain wrapped C or C++ code.

- **Easy**—It is very easy to get up to speed and begin writing Python programs. The clear, readable syntax makes applications simple to create and debug.

- **Power**—There are new extensions being written to Python all the time for things such as database access, audio/video editing, GUI, web development, and so on.

- **Dynamic**—Python is one of the most flexible languages. It's easy to get creative with code to solve design and development issues.

- **Open Source**—Python is an open source language, which means it can be freely used and distributed.

Invoking the Interpreter

Python scripts are executed by a Python interpreter. On most systems, you can start the Python interpreter by executing the python command at a console prompt. However, this can vary based on the system and development environment you have set up. This section discusses the standard methods to invoke the interpreter to execute Python statements and script files.

Invoking the interpreter without passing a script file as a parameter brings up the following prompt:

```
bwd-linux:/book # python
Python 2.4.2 (#1, Apr  9 2006, 19:25:19)
[GCC 4.1.0 (SUSE Linux)] on linux2
Type "help", "copyright", "credits" or
    "license" for more information.
>>>
```

The Python prompt is indicated by >>>. If you execute a command that requires more input, a ... prompt will be displayed. From the interpreter prompt, you can execute individual Python statements, as follows:

```
>>> print "Printing a String"
Printing a String
```

Invoking the interpreter with a script parameter, as shown next, begins execution of the script and continues until the script is finished. When the script is finished, the interpreter is no longer active.

```
bwd-linux:/book # python script.py
Executing a Script
bwd-linux:/book #
```

Scripts can also be executed from within the interpreter using the execfile(*script*) function built in to Python. The following example shows a script being executed using the execfile() function:

```
>>> execfile("script.py")
Executing a Script
>>>
```

Built-In Types

The built-in types that you will most frequently use in Python can be grouped into the categories listed in Table 1.1. The Type Name column shows the name that is associated with each built-in object type and can be used to determine whether an object is of a specific type using the `isinstance(object, typename)` function, as follows:

```
>>> s = "A Simple String"
>>> print isinstance(s, basestring)
True
>>> print isinstance(s, dict)
False
>>>
```

Table 1.1   **Common Built-In Python Types**

Type Category	Type Name	Description
None	types.NoneType	None object (null object)
Numbers	bool	Boolean True or False
	int	Integer
	long	Long integer
	float	Floating point
	complex	Complex number
Set	set	Mutable set
	frozenset	Immutable set
Sequences	str	Character string
	unicode	Unicode character string
	basestring	Base type of all strings
	list	List
	tuple	Tuple
	xrange	Immutable sequence

Table 1.1   **Continued**

Type Category	Type Name	Description
Mapping	`dict`	Dictionary
Files	`file`	File
Callable	`type`	Type for all built-ins
	`object`	Parent of all types and classes
	`types.Builtin FunctionType`	Built-in function
	`types.Builtin MethodType`	Built-in method
	`types. FunctionType`	User-defined function
	`types. InstanceType`	Class instance
	`types. MethodType`	Bound method
	`types.Unbounded MethodType`	Unbound method
Modules	`types. ModuleType`	Module
Classes	`object`	Parent of all classes
Type	`type`	Type for all built-ins

NOTE: The type module must be imported to use any of the type objects such as `type` and `types.ModuleType`.

None

The none type equates to a null object that has no value. The none type is the only object in Python that can be a null object. The syntax to use the none type in programs is simply `None`.

Numbers

The numeric types in Python are very straightforward. The `bool` type has two possible values: `True` and `False`. The `int` type internally stores whole numbers up to 32 bits. The `long` type can store numbers in a range that is limited only by the available memory of the machine. The `float` type uses native double-precision to store floating-point numbers up to 64 bits. The `complex` type stores values as a pair of floating-point numbers. The individual values are accessible using the `z.real` and `z.imag` attributes of the complex object.

Set

The set type represents an unordered collection of unique items. There are two basic types of sets: mutable and immutable. Mutable sets can be modified (items can be added or removed). Immutable sets cannot be changed after they are created.

NOTE: All items that are placed in a set must be of immutable type. Therefore, sets cannot contain items such as lists or dictionaries. However, they can include items such as strings and tuples.

Sequences

There are several sequence types in Python. Sequences are ordered and can be indexed by non-negative integers. Sequences are easily manipulated and can be made up of almost any Python object.

The two most common types of sequences by far are the string and list types. Chapter 2, "Manipulating Strings," discusses creating and using the string type. Chapter 3, "Managing Data Types," discusses the most common types of sequences and how to create and manipulate them.

Mapping

The mapping type represents two collections of objects. The first collection is a set of key objects that index the second collection that contains a set of value objects. Each key object indexes a specific value object in the correlating set. The key object must be of an immutable type. The value object can be almost any Python object.

The dictionary is the only mapping type currently built in to Python. Chapter 3 discusses dictionaries and how to create and manipulate them.

Files

The file type is a Python object that represents an open file. Objects of the file type can be used to read and write data to and from the filesystem. Chapter 4, "Managing Files," discusses file type objects and includes some of the most common Python phrases to utilize them.

Callable

Objects of the callable type support Python's function call operation, meaning that they can be called as a function of the program. Several objects fall into the callable type. The most common are the functions built in to the Python language, user-defined functions, classes, and method instances.

NOTE: Classes are considered callable because the class is called to create a new instance of the class. Once a new instance of a class has been called, the method instances of the class become callable also.

Modules

The module type represents Python modules that have been loaded by the import statement. The import statement creates a module type object with the same name as the Python module; then, all objects within the module are added to the __dict__ attribute of the newly created module type object.

Objects from the module can be accessed directly using the dot syntax because it is translated into a dictionary lookup. This way, you can use module.object instead of accessing an attribute using module.__dict__ ("object") to access objects from the module.

For example, the math module has the numeric object pi; the following code loads the math module and accesses the pi object:

```
>>> import math
>>> print math.pi
3.14159265359
```

Understanding Python Syntax

The Python language has many similarities to Perl, C, and Java. However, there are some definite differences between the languages. This section is designed to quickly get you up to speed on the syntax that is expected in Python.

Using Code Indentation

One of the first caveats programmers encounter when learning Python is the fact that there are no braces to indicate blocks of code for class and function definitions or flow control. Blocks of code are denoted by line indentation, which is rigidly enforced.

The number of spaces in the indentation is variable, but all statements within the block must be indented the same amount. Both blocks in this example are fine:

```
if True:
    print "True"
else:
  print "False"
```

However, the second block in this example will generate an error:

```
if True:
    print "Answer"
    print "True"
else:
    print "Answer"
  print "False"
```

Creating Multiline Statements

Statements in Python typically end with a new line. Python does, however, allow the use of the line continuation character (\) to denote that the line should continue. For example:

```
total_sum = sum_item_one + \
```

```
            sum_item_two + \
            sum_item_three
```

Statements contained within the [], {}, or () brackets do not need to use the line continuation character. For example:

```
week_list = ['Monday', 'Tuesday', 'Wednesday',
             'Thursday', 'Friday']
```

Quotation

Python accepts single ('), double ("), and triple (''' or """) quotes to denote string literals, as long as the same type of quote starts and ends the string. The triple quotes can be used to span the string across multiple lines. For example, all the following are legal:

```
word = 'word'
sentence = "This is a sentence."
paragraph = """This is a paragraph. It is
made up of multiple lines and sentences."""
```

Formatting Strings

Python allows for strings to be formatted using a pre-defined format string with a list of variables. The following is an example of using multiple format strings to display the same data:

```
>>>list = ["Brad", "Dayley", "Python Phrasebook",
2006]

>>>letter = """
>>>Dear Mr. %s,\n
>>>Thank you for your %s book submission.
>>>You should be hearing from us in %d."""

>>>display = """
```

```
>>>Title: %s
>>>Author: %s, %s
>>>Date: %d"""

>>>record = "%s|%s|%s|%08d"

>>>print letter % (list[1], list[2], list[3])
Dear Mr. Dayley,
Thank you for your Python Phrasebook book submis-
sion.
You should be hearing from us in 2006.

>>>print display % (list[2], list[1], list[0],
list[3])
Title: Python Phrasebook
Author: Dayley, Brad
Date: 2006

>>>print record % (list[0], list[1], list[2],
list[3])
Brad|Dayley|Python Phrasebook|00002006
```

Using Python Flow Control Statements

Python supports the if, else, and elif statements for conditional execution of code. The syntax is if *expression*: *block*. If the expression evaluates to true, execute the block of code. The following code shows an example of a simple series of if blocks:

```
if x = True:
    print "x is True"
elif y = true:
    print "y is True"
else:
    print "Both are False"
```

Python supports the `while` statement for conditional looping. The syntax is `while` *expression*: *block*. While the expression evaluates to true, execute the block in looping fashion. The following code shows an example of a conditional `while` loop:

```
x = 1
while x < 10:
    x += 1
```

Python also supports the `for` statement for sequential looping. The syntax is `for` *item in sequence*: *block*. Each loop item is set to the next item in the sequence, and the block of code is executed. The `for` loop continues until there are no more items left in the sequence. The following code shows several different examples of sequential `for` loops.

The first example uses a string as the sequence to create a list of characters in the string:

```
>>>word = "Python"
>>>list = []
>>>for ch in word:
>>>    list.append(ch)
>>>print list
['P', 'y', 't', 'h', 'o', 'n']
```

This example uses the `range()` function to create a temporary sequence of integers the size of a list so the items in the list can be added to a string in order:

```
>>>string = ""
>>>for i in range(len(list)):
>>>    string += list[i]
>>>print string
Python
```

This example uses the `enumerate(string)` function to create a temporary sequence. The `enumerate` function returns the enumeration in the form of (0, s[0]), (1, s[1]), and so on, until the end of the sequence `string`, so the `for` loop can assign both the i and ch value for each iteration to create a dictionary:

```
>>>dict = {}
>>>for i,ch in enumerate(string):
>>>    dict[i] = ch
>>>print dict
{0: 'P', 1: 'y', 2: 't', 3: 'h', 4: 'o', 5: 'n'}
```

This example uses a dictionary as the sequence to display the dictionary contents:

```
>>>for key in dict:
>>>    print key, '=', dict[key]
0 = P
1 = y
2 = t
3 = h
4 = o
5 = n
```

The Python language provides `break` to stop execution and break out of the current loop. Python also includes `continue` to stop execution of the current iteration and start the next iteration of the current loop. The following example shows the use of the `break` and `continue` statements:

```
>>>word = "Pithon Phrasebook"
>>>string = ""
>>>for ch in word:
>>>    if ch == 'i':
>>>        string += 'y'
>>>        continue
>>>    if ch == ' ':
>>>        break
>>>    string += ch
>>>print string
Python
```

> **NOTE:** An else statement can be added after a for or
> while loop just the same as an if statement. The
> else is executed after the loop successfully completes
> all iterations. If a break is encountered, the else state-
> ment is not executed.

There is currently no switch statement in Python.
Often this is not a problem and can be handled
through a series of if-elif-else statements. However,
there are many other ways to handle the deficiency.
The following example shows how to create a simple
switch statement in Python:

```
>>>def a(s):
>>>    print s
>>>def switch(ch):
>>>    try:
>>>       {'1': lambda : a("one"),
>>>        '2': lambda : a("two"),
>>>        '3': lambda : a("three"),
>>>        'a': lambda : a("Letter a")
>>>       }[ch]()
>>>    except KeyError:
>>>        a("Key not Found")
>>>switch('1')
one
>>>switch('a')
Letter a
>>>switch('b')
Key not Found
```

Python Objects, Modules, Classes, and Functions

This section is designed to help you understand the
basic concepts of objects, modules, classes, and functions

in the Python language. This section assumes that you have a basic understanding of object-oriented languages and is designed to provide the information to jump into Python and begin using and creating complex modules and classes.

Using Objects

The Python language is tightly wrapped around the object concept. Every piece of data stored and used in the Python language is an object. Lists, strings, dictionaries, numbers, classes, files, modules, and functions are all objects.

Every object in Python has an identity, a type, and a value. The *identity* points to the object's location in memory. The *type* describes the representation of the object to Python (see Table 1.1). The *value* of the object is simply the data stored inside.

The following example shows how to access the identity, type, and value of an object programmatically using the id(*object*), type(*object*), and variable name, respectively:

```
>>> l = [1,2,3]
>>> print id(l)
9267480
>>> print type(l)
<type 'list'>
>>> print l
[1, 2, 3]
```

After an object is created, the identity and type cannot be changed. If the object's value can be changed, it is considered a mutable object; if the value cannot be changed, it is considered an immutable object.

Some objects may also have attributes and methods.
Attributes are values associated with the object. *Methods*
are callable functions that perform an operation on the
object. Attributes and methods of an object can be
accessed using the following dot '.' syntax:

```
>>> class test(object):
...     def printNum(self):
...         print self.num
...
>>> t = test()
>>> t.num = 4
>>> t.printNum()
4
```

Using Modules

The entire Python language is built up of modules.
These modules are Python files that come from the
core modules delivered with the Python language,
modules created by third parties that extend the
Python language, and modules that you write yourself.
Large applications or libraries that incorporate several
modules are typically bundled into packages. Packages
allow several modules to be bundled under a single
name.

Modules are loaded into a Python program using the
`import` statement. When a module is imported, a namespace for the module, including all objects in the
source file, is created; the code in the source file is executed; and a module object with the same name as the
source file is created to provide access to the namespace.

There are several different ways to import modules.
The following examples illustrate some of the different
methods.

Modules can be imported directly using the package or module name. Items in submodules must be accessed explicitly including the full package name.

```
>>> import os
>>> os.path.abspath(".")
'C:\\books\\python'
```

Modules can be imported directly using the module name, but the namespace should be named something different. Items in submodules must be accessed explicitly including the full package name:

```
>>> import os as computer
>>> computer.path.abspath(".")
'C:\\books\\python'
```

Modules can be imported using the module name within the package name. Items in submodules must be accessed explicitly including the full package name:

```
>>> import os.path
>>> os.path.abspath(".")
'C:\\books\\python'
```

Modules can be imported by importing the modules specifically from the package. Items in submodules can be accessed implicitly without the package name:

```
>>> from os import path
>>> path.abspath(".")
'C:\\books\\python'
```

NOTE: Python includes a `reload(module)` function that reloads a module. This can be extremely useful during development if you need to update a module and reload it without terminating your program. However, objects created before the module is reloaded are not updated, so you must be careful in handling those objects.

Understanding Python Classes

Python classes are basically a collection of attributes and methods. Classes are typically used for one of two purposes: to create a whole new user-defined data type or to extend the capabilities of an existing one. This section assumes that you have a fair understanding of classes from C, Java, or another object-oriented language.

In Python, classes are extremely easy to define and *instantiate* (create new class object). Use the `class name(object)`: statement to define a new class, where the *name* is your own user-defined object type and the *object* specifies the Python object from which to inherit.

NOTE: Class inheritance in Python is similar to that in Java, C, and other object-oriented languages. The methods and attributes of the parent class will be available from the child, and any methods or attributes with the same name in the child will override the parents'.

All code contained in the block following the `class` statement will be executed each time the class is instantiated. The code sample testClass.py illustrates how to create a basic class in Python. The `class` statement sets the name of the class type and inherits from the base `object` class.

NOTE: The `class` statement only defines the class object type; it does not create a class object. The class object will still need to be created by calling the class directly.

The __init__() function overrides the method inherited from the object class and will be called when the class is instantiated. The class is instantiated by calling it directly: `tc = testClass("Five")`. When the class is called directly, an instance of the class object is returned.

NOTE: You can specify any necessary parameters to the __init__() function as long as you provide the parameters when calling the class to create a class object.

```
class testClass(object):
    print "Creating New Class\n===================="
    number=5
    def __init__(self, string):
        self.string = string
    def printClass(self):
        print "Number = %d"% self.number
        print "String = %s"% self.string

tc = testClass("Five")
tc.printClass()
tc.number = 10
tc.string = "Ten"
tc.printClass()
```

testClass.py

```
Creating New Class
====================
Number = 5
String = Five
Number = 10
String = Ten
```

Output from testClass.py code

NOTE: You need to use the `self.` prefix inside the class when referencing the attributes and methods of the class. Also, `self` is listed as the first argument in each of the class methods; however, it does not actually need to be specified when calling the method.

Using Functions

Defining and calling functions in Python is typically pretty easy; however, it can become extremely convoluted. The best thing to keep in mind is that functions are objects in the Python language and the parameters that are passed are really "applied" to the function object.

To create a function, use the `def functionname(parameters):` statement, and then define the function in the following code block. Once the function has been defined, you can call it by specifying the function name and passing the appropriate parameters.

That being said, the following paragraphs show some of the different ways to accomplish that simple task for the function shown here:

```python
def fun(name, location, year=2006):
    print "%s/%s/%d" % (name, location, year)
```

- The first example shows the function being called by passing the parameter values in order. Notice that the `year` parameter has a default value set in the function definition, which means that this parameter can be omitted and the default value will be used.

  ```python
  >>>fun("Teag", "San Diego")
  Teag/San Diego/2006
  ```

- The next example shows passing the parameters by name. The advantage of passing parameters by name is that the order in which they appear in the parameter list does not matter.

```
>>>fun(location="L.A.", year=2004, name="Caleb" )
Caleb/L.A./2004
```

- This example illustrates the ability to mix different methods of passing the parameters. In the example, the first parameter is passed as a value, and the second and third are passed as an assignment.

```
>>>fun("Aedan", year=2005, location="London")
Aedan/London/2005
```

- Parameters can also be passed as a tuple using the * syntax, as shown in this example. The items in the tuple must match the parameters that are expected by the function.

```
>>>tuple = ("DaNae", "Paris", 2003)
>>>fun(*tuple)
DaNae/Paris/2003
```

- Parameters can also be passed as a dictionary using the ** syntax, as shown in this example. The entries in the dictionary must match the parameters that are expected by the function.

```
>>>dictionary = {'name':'Brendan',
'location':'Orlando', 'year':1999}
>>>fun(**dictionary)
Brendan/Orlando/1999
```

- Values can be returned from functions using the return statement. If a function has no return statement, a None object is returned. The following example shows a simple square function that accepts a number and returns the square of the number:

```
>>> def square(x):
...      return x*x
...
>>> print square(3)
9
```

NOTE: Functions can be treated as any other Python object. In addition to being called, they can be assigned as a value to a list or dictionary, passed as an argument, returned as a value, and so on.

- The lambda operator built in to the Python language provides a method to create anonymous functions. This makes it easier to pass simple functions as parameters or assign them to variable names. The lambda operator uses the following syntax to define the function:

```
lambda <args> : <expression>
```

The term *args* refers to a list of arguments that get passed to the function. The term *expression* can be any legal Python expression. The following code shows an example of using the lambda operator to assign an anonymous function to a variable:

```
>>>bigger = lambda a, b : a > b
>>>print bigger(1,2)
False
>>>print bigger(2,1)
True
```

Namespaces and Scoping

Scoping in Python revolves around the concept of namespaces. *Namespaces* are basically dictionaries containing the names and values of the objects within a given scope. There are four basic types of namespaces that you will be dealing with: the global, local, module, and class namespaces

Global namespaces are created when a program begins execution. The global namespace initially includes built-in information about the module being executed. As new objects are defined in the global namespace scope, they are added to the namespace. The global namespace is accessible from all scopes, as shown in the example where the global value of x is retrieved using globals()["x"].

NOTE: You can look at the global namespace using the globals() function, which returns a dictionary object that includes all entries in the global namespace.

Local namespaces are created when a function is called. Local namespaces are nested with functions as they are nested. Name lookups begin in the most nested namespace and move out to the global namespaces.

The global statement forces names to be linked to the global namespace rather than to the local namespace. In the sample code, we use the global statement to force the name x to point to the global namespace. When x is changed, the global object will be modified.

NOTE: Although objects can be seen in outer nested namespaces, only the most local and global namespaces can be modified. In the sample code, the variable b from fun can be referenced for value in the sub function; however, modifying its value in sub would not change the value in fun.

```python
x = 1
def fun(a):
    b=3
    x=4
    def sub(c):
        d=b
        global x
        x = 7
        print ("Nested Function\n=================")
        print locals()

    sub(5)
    print ("\nFunction\n=================")
    print locals()
    print locals()["x"]
    print globals()["x"]

print ("\nGlobals\n=================")
print globals()

fun(2)
```

scope.py

```
Globals
=================
{'x': 1,
 '__file__':
```

```
'C:\\books\\python\\CH1\\code\\scope.py',
 'fun': <function fun at 0x008D7570>,
 't': <class '__main__.t'>,
 'time': <module 'time' (built-in)>,. . .}


Nested Function
=================
{'c': 5, 'b': 3, 'd': 3}

Function
=================
{'a': 2, 'x': 4, 'b': 3, 'sub':
    <function sub at 0x008D75F0>}
4
7
```

Output from scope.py code

The module namespace is created when a module is imported and the objects within the module are read. The module namespace can be accessed using the .__dict__ attribute of the module object. Objects in the module namespace can be accessed directly using the module name and dot "." syntax. The example shows this by calling the localtime() function of the time module:

```
>>>import time
>>>print time.__dict__
{'ctime': <built-in function ctime>,
 'clock': <built-in function clock>,
 ... 'localtime': <built-in function localtime>}
>>> print time.localtime()
(2006, 8, 10, 14, 32, 39, 3, 222, 1)
```

The class namespace is similar to the module namespace; however, it is created in two parts. The first part is created when the class is defined, and the second part is created when the class is instantiated. The

module namespace can also be accessed using the
.__dict__ attribute of the class object.

NOTE: Notice in the sample code that x resides in
t.__dict__ and double resides in tClass__dict__, yet
both are accessible using the dot syntax of the instantiated class object.

Objects in the class namespace can be accessed directly
using the module name and dot "." syntax. The example
shows this in the print t.x and t.double() statements:

```
>>>class tClass(object):
>>>    def __init__(self, x):
>>>        self.x = x
>>>    def double(self):
>>>        self.x += self.x
>>>t = tClass (5)
>>>print t.__dict__
{'x': 5}
>>>print tClass.__dict__
{'__module__': '__main__',
 'double': <function double at 0x008D7570>, . . . }
>>>print t.x
5
>>>t.double()
>>>print t.x
5
```

Error Handling

Error handling in Python is done through the use of
exceptions that are caught in try blocks and handled
in except blocks. If an error is encountered, a try block
code execution is stopped and transferred down to the
except block, as shown in the following syntax:

```
try:
    f = open("test.txt")
except IOError:
    print "Cannot open file."
```

The exception type value refers to either one of the built-in Python exceptions or a custom-defined exception object. The error value is a variable to capture the data returned by the exception.

NOTE: The try block also supports the use of an else block after the last except block. The else block is executed if the try block finishes without receiving an exception.

In addition to using an except block after the try block, you can also use the finally block. The code in the finally block will be executed regardless of whether an exception occurs. If no exception occurs, the finally block will be executed after the try block. If an exception occurs, the execution immediately is transferred to the finally block, and then the exception continues until it is handled. The following code shows an example of using finally to force a file to be closed even if an exception occurs:

```
f = open("test.txt")
try:
    f.write(data)
    . . .
finally:
    f.close()
```

You can raise an exception in your own program by using the raise exception [, value] statement. The value of exception is one of the built-in Python exceptions or a custom-defined exception object. The value of *value* is a Python object that you create to give details about the exception. Raising an exception breaks current code execution and returns the exception back until it is handled. The following example shows how to raise a generic RuntimeError exception with a simple text message value:

```
raise RuntimeError, "Error running script"
```

NOTE: If the exception is not handled, the program terminates and a trace of the exception is sent to sys.stderr.

Using System Tools

One of the most useful features of the Python language is the set of modules that provide access to the local computer system. These modules provide access to such things as the filesystem, OS, and shell, as well as various system functions.

This section discusses using the os, sys, platform, and time modules to access some of the more commonly used system information.

os Module

The os module provides a portable platform-independent interface to access common operating services, allowing you to add OS-level support to your programs. The following examples illustrate some of the most common uses of the os module.

The os.path.abspath(*path*) function of the os module returns a string version of the absolute path of the path specified. Because abspath takes into account the

current working directory, the . and .. directory
options will work as shown next:

```
>>>print os.path.abspath(".")
>>>C:\books\python\ch1\
print os.path.abspath("..")
C:\books\python\
```

The os.path module provides the exists(*path*),
isdir(*path*), and isfile(*path*) function to check for
the existence of files and directories, as shown here:

```
>>>print os.path.exists("/books/python/ch1")
True
>>>print os.path.isdir("/books/python/ch1")
True
>>>print os.path.isfile("/books/python/ch1/ch1.doc")
True
```

The os.chdir(*path*) function provides a simple way of
changing the current working directory for the program, as follows:

```
>>>os.chdir("/books/python/ch1/code")
>>>print os.path.abspath(".")
C:\books\python\CH1\code
```

The os.environ attribute contains a dictionary of environmental variables. You can use this dictionary as
shown next to access the environmental variables of
the system:

```
>>>print os.environ['PATH']
C:\WINNT\system32;C:\WINNT;C:\Python24
```

The os.system(*command*) function will execute a system
function as if it were in a subshell, as shown with the
following dir command:

```
>>>os.system("dir")
```

```
Volume Serial Number is 98F3-A875
 Directory of C:\books\python\ch1\code
08/11/2006   02:10p      <DIR>            .
08/11/2006   02:10p      <DIR>            ..
08/10/2006   04:00p                  405 format.py
08/10/2006   10:27a                  546 function.py
08/10/2006   03:07p                  737 scope.py
08/11/2006   02:58p                  791 sys_tools.py
               4 File(s)        3,717 bytes
               2 Dir(s)   7,880,230,400 bytes free
```

Python provides a number of exec type functions to execute applications on the native system. The following example illustrates using the os.execvp(*path*, *args*) function to execute the application update.exe with the command-line parameter of -verbose:

```
>>>os.execvp("update.exe", ["-verbose"])
```

sys Module

The sys module provides an interface to access the environment of the Python interpreter. The following examples illustrate some of the most common uses of the sys module.

The argv attribute of the sys module is a list. The first item in the argv list is the path to the module; the rest of the list is made up of arguments that were passed to the module at the beginning of execution. The sample code shows how to use the argv list to access command-line parameters passed to a Python module:

```
>>>print sys.argv
['C:\\books\\python\\CH1\\code\\print_it.py',
'text']
>>>print sys.argv[1]
text
```

The stdin attribute of the sys module is a file object that gets created at the start of code execution. In the following sample code, text is read from stdin (in this case, the keyboard, which is the default) using the readline() function:

```
>>>text = sys.stdin.readline()
>>>print text
Input Text
```

The sys module also has the stdout and stderr attributes that point to files used for standard output and standard error output. These files default to writing to the screen. The following sample code shows how to redirect the standard output and standard error messages to a file rather than to the screen:

```
>>>sOUT = sys.stdout
>>>sERR = sys.stderr
>>>sys.stdout = open("ouput.txt", "w")
>>>sys.stderr = sys.stdout
>>>sys.stdout = sOUT
>>>sys.stderr = sERR
```

platform Module

The platform module provides a portable interface to information about the platform on which the program is being executed. The following examples illustrate some of the most common uses of the platform module.

The platform.architecture() function returns the *(bits, linkage)* tuple that specifies the number of bits for the system word size and linkage information about the Python executable:

```
>>>print platform.architecture()
('32bit', '')
```

The `platform.python_version()` function returns the version of the Python executable for compatibility purposes:

```
>>>print platform.python_version()
2.4.2
```

The `platform.uname()` function returns a tuple in the form of (*system*, *node*, *release*, *version*, *machine*, *processor*). *System* refers to which OS is currently running, *node* refers to the host name of the machine, *release* refers to the major release of the OS, *version* refers to a string representing OS release information, and *machine* and *processor* refer to the hardware platform information.

```
>>>print platform.uname()
('Linux', 'bwd-linux', '2.6.16-20-smp',
 '#1 SMP Mon Apr 10 04:51:13 UTC 2006',
 'i686', 'i686')
```

time Module

The time module provides a portable interface to time functions on the system on which the program is executing. The following examples illustrate some of the most common uses of the time module.

The `time.time()` function returns the current system time in terms of the number of seconds since the UTC (Coordinated Universal Time). This value is typically collected at various points in the program and is used in delta operations to determine the amount of time since an event occurred.

```
>>>print time.time()
1155333864.11
```

The time.localtime(*secs*) function returns the time, specified by secs since the UTC, in the form of a tuple (*year, month, day, hour, minute, second, day of week, day of year, daylight savings*). If no time is specified, the current time is used as follows:

```
>>>print time.localtime()
(2006, 8, 11, 16, 4, 24, 4, 223, 1)
```

The time.ctime(*secs*) function returns the time, specified by *secs* since the UTC, as a formatted, printable string. If no time is specified, the current time is used as shown here:

```
>>>print time.ctime()
Fri Aug 11 16:04:24 2006
```

The time.clock() function returns the current CPU time as a floating-point number that can be used for various timing functions:

```
>>>print time.clock()
5.02857206712e-006
```

The time.sleep(*secs*) function forces the current process to sleep for the number of seconds specified by the floating-point number *secs*:

```
>>>time.sleep(.5)
```

2

Manipulating Strings

One of the most common and important functions of the Python language is to process and manipulate large amounts of text when implementing scripts, parsing XML/HTML, and interfacing with databases. For that reason, Python includes extremely dynamic and powerful string manipulation methods.

The phrases in this chapter are intended to give you a quick start into manipulating strings using the Python language. Although this chapter is not comprehensive, it tries to cover both the most commonly used functionality such as string comparisons, searching, and formatting, as well as some of the more powerful and dynamic functionality such as using strings as executable code, interpolating variables in strings, and evaluating strings as Python expressions.

Comparing Strings

```python
if cmpStr.upper() == upperStr.upper():
    print upperStr + " Matches " + cmpStr
```

Comparing strings in Python is best accomplished using a simple logical operation. For example, to determine whether a string matches another string exactly, you would use the `is equal` or `==` operation. You can also use other logical operations such as `>=` or `<` to determine a sort order for several strings.

Python provides several methods for string objects that help when comparing. The most commonly used are the `upper()` and `lower()` methods, which return a new string that is all upper- or lowercase, respectively.

Another useful method is the `capitalize()` method, which returns a new string with the first letter capitalized. There is also a `swapcase()` that will return a new string with exactly the opposite casing for each character.

```python
cmpStr = "abc"
upperStr = "ABC"
lowerStr = "abc"

print "Case Sensitive Compare"
if cmpStr == lowerStr:
    print lowerStr + " Matches " + cmpStr

if cmpStr == upperStr:
    print upperStr + " Matches " + cmpStr

print "\nCase In-Sensitive Compare"
if cmpStr.upper() == lowerStr.upper():
    print lowerStr + " Matches " + cmpStr

if cmpStr.upper() == upperStr.upper():
    print upperStr + " Matches " + cmpStr
```

comp_str.py

```
Case Sensitive Compare
abc Matches abc

Case In-Sensitive Compare
abc Matches abc
ABC Matches abc
```

Output from comp_str.py code

Joining Strings

```
print "Words:" + word1 + word2 + word3 + word4
print "List: " + ' '.join(wordList)
```

Strings can be joined together using a simple add operation, formatting the strings together, or using the join() method. Using either the + or += operation is the simplest method to implement and start off with. The two strings are simply appended to each other.

Formatting strings together is accomplished by defining a new string with string format codes, %s, and then adding additional strings as parameters to fill in each string format code. This can be extremely useful, especially when the strings need to be joined in a complex format.

The fastest way to join a list of strings is to use the join(wordList) method to join all the strings in a list. Each string, starting with the first, is added to the existing string in order. The join method can be a little tricky at first because it essentially performs a string+=list[x] operation on each iteration through the list of strings. This results in the string being appended as a prefix to each item in the list. This actually becomes extremely useful if you want to add spaces between the words in the list because you simply define a string as a single space and then implement the join method from that string:

```
word1 = "A"
word2 = "few"
word3 = "good"
word4 = "words"
wordList = ["A", "few", "more", "good", "words"]

#simple Join
print "Words:" + word1 + word2 + word3 + word4
print "List: " + ' '.join(wordList)

#Formatted String
sentence = ("First: %s %s %s %s." %
(word1,word2,word3,word4))
print sentence

#Joining a list of words
sentence = "Second:"
for word in wordList:
    sentence += " " + word
sentence += "."
print sentence
```

join_str.py

```
Words:Afewgoodwords
List: A few more good words
First: A few good words.
Second: A few more good words.
```

Output from join_str.py code

Splitting Strings

```
print sentence.split()
print entry.split(':')
print paragraph.splitlines(1)
```

The split(*separator*) and splitlines(*keeplineends*) methods are provided by Python to split strings into substrings. The split method searches a string, splits it on each occurrence of the separator character, and subdivides it into a list of strings. If no separator character is specified, the split method will split the string at each occurrence of a whitespace character (space, tab, newline, and so on).

The splitlines method splits the string at each newline character into a list of strings. This can be extremely useful when you are parsing a large amount of text. The splitlines method accepts one argument that is a Boolean true or false to determine whether the newline character should be kept.

```
sentence = "A Simple Sentence."

paragraph = "This is a simple paragraph.\n\
It is made up of of multiple\n\
lines of text."

entry = \
  "Name:Brad Dayley:Occupation:Software Engineer"

print sentence.split()
print entry.split(':')
print paragraph.splitlines(1)
```

split_str.py

```
['A', 'Simple', 'Sentence.']
['Name', 'Brad Dayley', 'Occupation',
 'Software Engineer']
['This is a simple paragraph.\n',
 'It is made up of of multiple\n',
 'lines of text.']
```

Output from split_str.py code

Searching Strings for Substrings

```
print searchStr.find("Red")
print searchStr.rfind("Blue")
print searchStr.index("Blue")
print searchStr.index("Blue",8)
```

The two most common ways to search for a substring contained inside another string are the find(sub, [, start, [,end]]) and index(sub, [, start, [,end]]) methods.

The index method is faster than the find method; however, if the substring is not found in the string, an exception is thrown. If the find method fails to find the substring, a -1 is returned. The find and index methods accept a search string as the first argument. The area of the string that is searched can be limited by specifying the optional start and/or end index. Only characters within those indexes will be searched.

Python also provides the rfind and rindex methods. These methods work in a similar manner as the find and index methods; however, they look for the right-most occurrence of the substring.

```
searchStr =
 "Red Blue Violet Green Blue Yellow Black"

print searchStr.find("Red")
print searchStr.rfind("Blue")
print searchStr.find("Blue")
print searchStr.find("Teal")
print searchStr.index("Blue")
print searchStr.index("Blue",20)
print searchStr.rindex("Blue")
print searchStr.rindex("Blue",1,18)
```

search_str.py

```
0
22
4
-1
4
22
22
4
```

Output from search_str.py code

Search and Replace in Strings

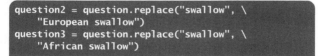

```
question2 = question.replace("swallow", \
    "European swallow")
question3 = question.replace("swallow", \
    "African swallow")
```

The native string type in Python provides a
replace(*old*, *new*, *maxreplace*) method to replace a
specific substring with new text. The replace method
accepts a search string as the first argument and
replacement string as the second argument. Each

occurrence of the search string will be replaced with the new string. Optionally, you can specify a maximum number of times to perform the replace operation as the third argument.

```
question = "What is the air speed velocity of \
    an unlaiden swallow?"
print question
question2 = question.replace("swallow", \
    "European swallow")
print question2
question3 = question.replace("swallow", \
    "African swallow")
print question3
```

replace_str.py

```
What is the air speed velocity of an unlaiden
swallow?
What is the air speed velocity of an unlaiden
European swallow?
What is the air speed velocity of an unlaiden
African swallow?
```

Output from replace_str.py code

Searching Strings for Specific Endings/Beginnings

```
if f.endswith('.py'):
    print "Python file: " + f
elif f.endswith('.txt'):
    print "Text file: " + f
```

The endswith(suffix, [, *start*, [,*end*]]) and startswith(prefix, [, *start*, [,*end*]]) methods provide a simple and safe way to determine whether a string begins or ends with a specific prefix or suffix, respectively. The first argument is a string used to compare to the prefix or suffix of the string. The endswith and startswith methods are dynamic enough for you to limit the search to within a specific range of the string using the *start* and/or *end* arguments.

NOTE: The endswith and startswith methods are extremely useful when parsing file lists for extensions or filenames.

```python
import os

for f in os.listdir('C:\\txtfiles'):
    if f.endswith('.py'):
        print "Python file: " + f
    elif f.endswith('.txt'):
        print "Text file: " + f
```

end_str.py

```
Python file: comp_str.py
Python file: end_str.py
Python file: eval_str.py
Python file: join_str.py
Text file: output.txt
Python file: replace_str.py
Python file: search_str.py
Python file: split_str.py
Python file: trim_str.py
Python file: unicode_str.py
Python file: var_str.py
```

Output from end_str.py code

Trimming Strings

```
str(len(badSentence.rstrip(' ')))
print badSentence.lstrip('\t')
print badParagraph.strip((' ?!\t'))
```

Common problems when parsing text are leftover characters at the beginning or end of the string. Python provides several strip methods to remove those characters. The strip([*chrs*]), lstrip([*chrs*]), and rstrip([*chrs*]) methods accept a list of characters as the only argument and return a new string with those characters trimmed from either the start, end, or both ends of the string.

NOTE: The strip method will remove the specified characters from both the beginning and end of the string. The lstrip and rstrip methods remove the characters only from the beginning or end of the string, respectively.

```
import string
badSentence = "\t\tThis sentence has problems.    "

badParagraph = "\t\tThis paragraph \nhas even \
    more \nproblems.!?    "

#Strip trailing spaces
print "Length = " + str(len(badSentence))
print "Without trailing spaces = " + \
    str(len(badSentence.rstrip(' ')))

#Strip tabs
print "\nBad:\n" + badSentence
print "\nFixed:\n" + badSentence.lstrip('\t')

#Strip leading and trailing characters
```

```
print "\nBad:\n" + badParagraph
print "\nFixed:\n" + badParagraph.strip((' ?!\t'))
```

trim_str.py

```
Length = 32
Without trailing spaces = 29

Bad:
                This sentence has problems.

Fixed:
This sentence has problems.

Bad:
                This paragraph
has even more
problems.!?

Fixed:
This paragraph
has even more
problems.
```

Output from trim_str.py code

Aligning/Formatting Strings

```
print "Chapter " + str(x) + \
    str(chapters[x].rjust(15,'.')
print "\nHex String: " + hexStr.upper().ljust(8,'0')
print "Chapter %d %15s" % (x,str(chapters[x]))
```

One of the biggest advantages of the Python language is its capability to process and manipulate strings quickly and effectively. The native string type implements the rjust(width [, *fill*]) and ljust(width [, *fill*]) methods to quickly justify the text in a string a specific width to the right or left, respectively. The optional *fill* argument to the rjust and ljust methods will fill the space created by the justification with the specified character.

Another extremely useful part of Python's string management is the capability to create complex string formatting on the fly by creating a format string and passing arguments to that string using the % operator. This results in a new formatted string that can be used in a string assignment, passed as an argument, or used in a print statement.

```
chapters = {1:5, 2:46, 3:52, 4:87, 5:90}
hexStr = "3f8"

#Right justify
print "Hex String: " + hexStr.upper().rjust(8,'0')
print
for x in chapters:
    print "Chapter " + str(x) + \
        str(chapters[x]).rjust(15,'.')


#Left justify
print "\nHex String: " + hexStr.upper().ljust(8,'0')

#String format
print
for x in chapters:
    print "Chapter %d %15s" % (x,str(chapters[x]))
```

format_str.py

```
Hex String: 000003F8
```

```
Chapter 1.............5
Chapter 2............46
Chapter 3............52
Chapter 4............87
Chapter 5............90

Hex String: 3F800000

Chapter 1              5
Chapter 2              46
Chapter 3              52
Chapter 4              87
Chapter 5              90
```

Output from format_str.py code

Executing Code Inside Strings

```
codeStr = "for card in cards: \
    print \"Card = \" + card"
exec(codeStr)
```

One of the most dynamic features of Python is the capability to evaluate a string that contains code and execute the code locally. The exec(*str* [,*globals* [,*locals*]]) function will execute Python code that is contained in the *str* string and return the result. Local and global variables can be added to the environment used to execute the code by specifying global and/or local dictionaries containing corresponding variable name and values.

The eval(*str* [,*globals* [,*locals*]]) function works in a similar manner to the exec function except that it only evaluates the string as a Python expression and returns the results.

```
cards = ['Ace', 'King', 'Queen', 'Jack']
codeStr = "for card in cards: \
    print \"Card = \" + card"
areaStr = "pi*(radius*radius)"

#Execute string
exec(codeStr)

#Evaluate string
print "\nArea = " + str(eval(areaStr, \
    {"pi":3.14}, {"radius":5}))
```

eval_str.py

```
Card = Ace
Card = King
Card = Queen
Card = Jack

Area = 78.5
```

Output from eval_str.py code

Interpolating Variables Inside Strings

```
s = string.Template("Variable v = $v")
for x in values:
    print s.substitute(v=x)
```

Python provides the capability to interpolate variables inside strings. This functionality provides the ability to create string templates and then apply variable values to them based on the state of an existing variable.

Interpolating variables is accomplished in two steps. The first step is to create a string template, using the `Template(string)` method, which includes the formatted text and properly placed variable names preceded by the $ character.

NOTE: To include a $ character in your template string use a double $$ set. The $$ will be replaced with a single $ when the template is applied.

Once the template has been created, the second step is to apply a variable value to the template using the `substitute(m, [, kwargs])` method of the `Template` class. The argument *m* can be a specific assignment, a dictionary of variable values, or a keyword list.

```
import string

values = [5, 3, 'blue', 'red']
s = string.Template("Variable v = $v")

for x in values:
    print s.substitute(v=x)
```

var_str.py

```
Variable v = 5
Variable v = 3
Variable v = blue
Variable v = red
```

Output from var_str.py code

Converting Unicode to Local Strings

```
print uniStr.encode('utf-8')
print uniStr.encode('utf-16')
print uniStr.encode('iso-8859-1')
asciiStr =asciiStr.translate( \
    string.maketrans('\xF1','n'), '')
print asciiStr.encode('ascii')
```

The Python language provides a simple encode(*encoding*) method to convert unicode strings to a local string for easier processing. The encoding method takes only encoding such as utf-8, utf-16, iso-8859-1, and ascii as its single argument and returns a string encoded in that format.

Strings can be converted to unicode by several different methods. One is to define the string as unicode by prefixing it with a u when assigning it to a variable. Another is to combine a unicode string with another string. The resulting string will be unicode. You can also use the decode(*encoding*) method to decode the string. The decode method returns a unicode form of the string.

NOTE: The ASCII encoding allows only for characters up to 128. If your string includes characters that are above that range, you will need to translate those characters before encoding the string to ASCII.

```
import string

locStr = "El "
uniStr = u"Ni\u00F1o"

print uniStr.encode('utf-8')
```

```
print uniStr.encode('utf-16')
print uniStr.encode('iso-8859-1')

#Combine local and unicode results
#in new unicode string
newStr = locStr+uniStr
print newStr.encode('iso-8859-1')


#ascii will error because character '\xF1'
#is out of range
asciiStr = newStr.encode('iso-8859-1')
asciiStr =asciiStr.translate(\
    string.maketrans('\xF1','n'), '')
print asciiStr.encode('ascii')
print newStr.encode('ascii')
```

unicode_str.py

```
NiÃ±o
ÿþN|I|ñ|o
Niño
El Niño
El Nino
Traceback (most recent call last):
  File "C:\books\python\CH2\code\unicode_str.py",
line 19, in ?
    print newStr.encode('ascii')
UnicodeEncodeError: 'ascii' codec can't encode
 character u'\xf1' in position 5: ordinal not in
 range(128)
```

Output from unicode_str.py code

Managing Data Types

Python has about two dozen data types built in to the interpreter. The three data types that you will need to understand the best and use the most to manage data are the list, tuple, and dictionary.

A *list* in Python is simply an ordered collection of objects. The objects can be named any legal Python name and the list can grow dynamically to support the addition of new objects. The objects in a list can be of different types and Python will keep track of the data type of objects in the background. Lists in Python are ordered sequence types. Elements of a list are accessible using a zero-based non-negative integer index.

A *tuple* in one sense is just a read-only version of a list. It is also an ordered sequence of objects. However, a tuple is *immutable*, meaning that items cannot be added to or removed from it.

A *dictionary* is an unordered collection of object pairs. The pair consists of a key object and a value object. The key object is used to look up the value of the value object. A dictionary acts similar to a hash table in

that the key is used to access the value objects within.
There is no order to a dictionary; therefore, items cannot be accessed by any indexing method.

This chapter discusses phrases that allow you to manage data using the list, tuple, and dictionary data types.

Defining a List

```
numList = [2000, 2003, 2005, 2006]
stringList = ["Essential", "Python", "Code"]
mixedList = [1, 2, "three", 4]
subList = ["Python", "Phrasebook", \
  ["Copyright", 2006]]
listList = [numList, stringList, mixedList, subList]
```

Defining a list in Python is a simple matter of assigning a number of Python objects to a variable name
using the = operator. The list needs to be enclosed in
square brackets and can include any makeup of Python
objects. A simple numeric list acts much like an array;
however, lists are much more dynamic and can include
many different types within the same list.

The code example in def_list.py demonstrates the cre-
ation of both homogeneous and heterogeneous lists.
Notice in the example that the lists include numbers,
strings, list definitions, and variable names.

```
numList = [2000, 2003, 2005, 2006]
stringList = ["Essential", "Python", "Code"]
mixedList = [1, 2, "three", 4]
subList = ["Python", "Phrasebook", \
  ["Copyright", 2006]]
listList = [numList, stringList, mixedList, subList]

for x in listList:
```

```
    for y in x:
        if isinstance(y, int):
            print y + 1
        if isinstance(y, basestring):
            print "String: " + y
```

def_list.py

```
2001
2004
2006
2007
String: Essential
String: Python
String: Code
2
3
String: three
5
String: Python
String: Phrasebook
```

Output from def_list.py code

Accessing a List

```
for x in numList:
    print x+1
print stringList[0] + ' ' + stringList[1] + ' ' + \
    stringList[2]
print stringList[-2]
if isinstance(subList, list):
    print subList[2][0]
```

Once a list is defined, the items in the list can be accessed using a zero-based index. The first item in the list is at index zero, the second at index one, and so on.

The code example in acc_list.py demonstrates access-ing all items of the list in order using the `for` keyword, as well as accessing the items in the list individually.

If an item in the list is a list object, you can access items in that list by adding an indexing bracket onto the end, similar to how you would access elements in a multidimensional array.

NOTE: Python enables you to use negative indices to access the list from the end rather than from the beginning. For example, to access the final item in a list, you would use an index of –1, an index of –2 to access the second to the last item in the list, and so on. This can be extremely useful if you have dynamic lists that change frequently.

```
numList = [2000, 2003, 2005, 2006]
stringList = ["Essential", "Python", "Code"]
mixedList = [1, 2, "three", 4]
subList = ["Python", "Phrasebook", ["Copyright",
2006]]
listList = [numList, stringList, mixedList, subList]


#All items
for x in numList:
    print x+1

#Specific items
print stringList[0] + ' ' + stringList[1] + ' ' + \
    stringList[2]

#Negative indices
```

```
print stringList[-2]

#Accessing items in sublists
if isinstance(subList, list):
    print subList[2][0]
```

acc_list.py

```
2001
2004
2006
2007
Essential Python Code
Python
Copyright
```

Output from acc_list.py code

Slicing a List

```
firstHalf = monthList[ : halfCount]
secondHalf = monthList[halfCount : ]
wordCount = len(firstHalf)
middleStart = wordCount/2
middleHalf = monthList[middleStart : \
    middleStart+halfCount]
```

A *slice* is a subset of a list. Python provides syntax that enables you to quickly grab specific slices of a list.

A slice can be obtained by referencing the list and specifying two indices (separated by a colon) to reference between instead of a single index number. The first index number represents the item in the list at which to start and the second represents the item in the list at which to end.

Slices are returned as a list type and can be accessed and assigned as you would any other list.

NOTE: Python enables you to use negative indices to index the end rather than the beginning when grabbing slices. For example, to access the final three items in a list, you would use the indices of –3 and –1.

```python
monthList = ["January", "February", "March", \
             "April", "May", "June", "July", \
             "August", "September", "October",\
             "November", "December"]

wordCount = len(monthList)
halfCount = wordCount/2

#Beginning slice
firstHalf = monthList[ : halfCount]
print firstHalf

#End slice
secondHalf = monthList[halfCount : ]
print secondHalf

#Middle slice
wordCount = len(firstHalf)
middleStart = wordCount/2
middleHalf = monthList[middleStart : \
    middleStart+halfCount]
print middleHalf


#Negative Indices
print monthList[-5 : -1]
```

slice_list.py

```
['January', 'February', 'March', 'April', 'May',
'June']
['July', 'August', 'September', 'October',
'November', 'December']
['April', 'May', 'June', 'July', 'August',
'September']
['August', 'September', 'October', 'November']
```

Output from slice_list.py code

Adding and Removing Items in a List

```
list1.append("Four")
list1.insert(2, "Two 1/2")
list1.extend(list2)
print list1.pop(2)
list1.remove("Five")
list1.remove("Six")
```

Items can be added to an existing list in several different ways, depending on what items you want to add to the list and where you want to add them.

The simplest way to add a single item to a list is to use the append(*item*) method. append takes a single item—which can be any Python object, including other lists—as the only parameter and adds it to the end of the list. If you specify a list as the parameter to the append method, that list is added as a single item in the current list.

Use the extend(*list*) method to add several items stored in another list all together at the same time. extend will accept only a list as an argument. Unlike the append method, each item in the new list will be appended as its own individual item to the old list.

The extend and append methods will add items only to
the end of the list. Use the insert(*index*, *item*)
method to insert an item in the middle of the list. The
insert method accepts a single object as the second
parameter and inserts it into the list at the index specified by the first argument.

Items can be removed from a list in one of two ways.
The first way is to use the pop(*index*) method to
remove the item by its index. The pop method removes
the object from the list and then returns it.

The second way to remove an item from a list is to use
the remove(*item*) method. The remove method will search
the list and remove the first occurrence of the item.

NOTE: You can also add one or more lists to an existing list by using the += operator.

```
list1 = ["One", "Two", "Three"]
list2 = ["Five", "Six"]

print list1

#Append item
list1.append("Four")
print list1

#Insert item at index
list1.insert(2, "Two 1/2")
print list1

#Extend with list
list1.extend(list2)
print list1

#Pop item by index
```

```
print list1.pop(2)
print list1

#Remove item
list1.remove("Five")
list1.remove("Six")
print list1

#Operators
list1 += list2
print list1
```

add_list.py

```
['One', 'Two', 'Three']
['One', 'Two', 'Three', 'Four']
['One', 'Two', 'Two 1/2', 'Three', 'Four']
['One', 'Two', 'Two 1/2', 'Three', 'Four',
'Five', 'Six']
Two 1/2
['One', 'Two', 'Three', 'Four', 'Five', 'Six']
['One', 'Two', 'Three', 'Four']
['One', 'Two', 'Three', 'Four', 'Five', 'Six']
```

Output from add_list.py code

Sorting a List

```
def keySort (x, y):
    xIndex = keyList.index(x)
    yIndex = keyList.index(y)
    return cmp(xIndex, yIndex)

letterList.sort()
letterList.sort(lambda x, y: keySort(x, y))
caseList.sort()
caseList.sort(key=str.lower)
letterList.reverse()
letterList.sort(reverse=1)
```

Items in a list can be sorted using the sort() method.
The basic sort method takes no arguments and sorts
the items based on the total value of each object. The
sort method actually modifies the order of the objects
in the list itself. This works as a simple and very effective way to sort simple lists.

The sort method can also accept a comparison function as an argument. The comparison function accepts
two arguments and must return a 1, 0, or −1 depending on whether the second argument is smaller, the
same size, or larger than the first argument.

The sort method can also accept a key function. The
key function should accept one argument that will be
used to extract a key from each object in the list. That
key will be used to sort the list rather than the value of
the object itself.

A list can be sorted in reverse order, by passing the
keyterm reverse as an argument to the sort method.
reverse is a Boolean, and if it is set to true, the list is
sorted in reverse order. The reverse keyterm can be
used in tandem with comparison and/or key functions.

NOTE: If you simply need to reverse the order of a list
without necessarily sorting it, use the reverse()
method. The reverse method accepts no arguments
and simply reverses the order of the items in the list.

```
keyList = ['a', 'c', 'b', 'y', 'z', 'x']
letterList = ['b', 'c', 'a', 'z', 'y', 'x']
caseList = ['d', 'B', 'F', 'A', 'E', 'c']

#Custom sort procedure
def keySort (x, y):
    xIndex = keyList.index(x)
```

```
    yIndex = keyList.index(y)
    return cmp(xIndex, yIndex)

print letterList

#Sort the list
letterList.sort()
print letterList

#Custom sort
letterList.sort(lambda x, y: keySort(x, y))
print letterList

#Key sort
print caseList
caseList.sort()
print caseList
caseList.sort(key=str.lower)
print caseList

#Reverse list
letterList.reverse()
print letterList

#Reverse sort
letterList.sort(reverse=1)
print letterList
```

sort_list.py

```
['b', 'c', 'a', 'z', 'y', 'x']
['a', 'b', 'c', 'x', 'y', 'z']
['a', 'c', 'b', 'y', 'z', 'x']
['d', 'B', 'F', 'A', 'E', 'c']
['A', 'B', 'E', 'F', 'c', 'd']
['A', 'B', 'c', 'd', 'E', 'F']
['x', 'z', 'y', 'b', 'c', 'a']
['z', 'y', 'x', 'c', 'b', 'a']
```

Output from sort_list.py code

Using Tuples

```python
hexStringChars = ('A', 'B', 'C', 'D', 'E', 'F')
hexStringNums = ('1', '2', '3', '4', '5', '6',\
                 '7', '8', '9', '0')
hexStrings = ["1FC", "1FG", "222", "Ten"]

for hexString in hexStrings:
    for x in hexString:
        if ((not x in hexStringChars) and
            (not x in hexStringNums)):
            print hexString + \
                " is not a hex string."
            break

tupleList = list(hexStringChars)
listTuple = tuple(hexStrings)
```

When working with lists in Python, it is a good idea
to understand the place that tuples have. Tuples are
similar to lists in that they are index-based collections
of objects. There is one major difference, however. The
contents of a tuple cannot be modified after the tuple
is initially defined. Tuples are defined similar to lists
except that they are encased in parentheses instead of
in brackets.

Tuples are very valuable because they are much faster
to access and use than lists. For example, the in operation works much faster on a tuple to determine
whether an object exists in the tuple. Tuples are also
valuable because you know the data contained in them
will always remain static. Tuples can also be used as
keys for dictionaries where lists cannot.

NOTE: The tuples must be made up of strings and/or
integers and cannot contain lists to be considered
immutable and used as dictionary keys.

Tuples can be converted into lists by using the list()
function. The list function returns a copy of the tuple
in an editable list form. In the same way, lists can be
converted into tuples using the tuple() function. The
tuple function returns a copy of the list in tuple form,
effectively giving you a frozen snapshot of the list.

```python
hexStringChars = ('A', 'B', 'C', 'D', 'E', 'F')
hexStringNums = ('1', '2', '3', '4', '5', '6',\
                 '7', '8', '9', '0')

hexStrings = ["1FC", "1FG", "222", "Ten"]

for hexString in hexStrings:
    for x in hexString:
        if ((not x in hexStringChars) and
            (not x in hexStringNums)):
            print hexString + \
                " is not a hex string."
            break

#Tuple to list
tupleList = list(hexStringChars)
print tupleList

#List to tuple
listTuple = tuple(hexStrings)
print listTuple
```

tuple.py

```
1FG is not a hex string.
Ten is not a hex string.
['A', 'B', 'C', 'D', 'E', 'F']
('1FC', '1FG', '222', 'Ten')
```

Output from tuple.py code

Constructing a Dictionary

```
numberDict = {1:'one', 2:'two', 3:'three', 4:'four'}
letterDict = {'vowel':['a','e','i','o','u'],\
              'consonant':['b','c','d','f']}
numbers = (1,2,3,4,5,6,7,8,9,0)
letters = ('a','b','c','d','e','f')
punct = ('.', '!', '?')
charSetDict = {numbers:[], letters:[], punct:[]}
```

Constructing a dictionary in Python is a simple matter of assigning a group of values with associated keys to a variable. Although the values can be any Python object, the keys must either be a number, string, or immutable tuple.

Simple dictionaries are made up of simple one-to-one, key-to-value relationships. However, you can construct very complex dictionaries that can have one-to-many and even many-to-many value relationships.

A one-to-many relationship can be accomplished by simply using list objects as the values in the dictionary.

The many-to-many relationship will take more thought and effort; however, this relationship can be accomplished by using tuples as the key objects and list objects as the value objects in the dictionary.

```
#Simple one to one dictionary
numberDict = {1:'one', 2:'two', 3:'three', 4:'four'}

#One to many dictionary
letterDict = {'vowel':['a','e','i','o','u'],\
              'consonant':['b','c','d','f']}

#Many to many dictionary
numbers = (1,2,3,4,5,6,7,8,9,0)
letters = ('a','b','c','d','e','f')
```

```
punct = ('.', '!', '?')
charSetDict = {numbers:[], letters:[], punct:[]}
```

def_dict.py

Adding a Value to a Dictionary

```
numbers = ('1','2','3','4','5','6','7','8','9','0')
letters = ('a','b','c','d','e','f')
punct = ('.', '!', '?')
charSetDict = {numbers:[], letters:[], punct:[]}
cSet = raw_input("Insert characters: ")
for c in cSet:
    for x in charSetDict.keys():
        if c in x:
            charSetDict[x].append(c)
            break;
charSetDict["Special"] = ['%', '$', '#']
charSetDict["Special"] = '><'
```

Adding values to a dictionary is really just setting up a key in the dictionary to correspond to a specific value. When assigning a value to the dictionary, if the key you specify does not already exist in the dictionary, the key is added to the dictionary and the value is assigned to it. If the key already exists in the dictionary, the value object currently assigned to the key will be replaced by the new value object.

The object type of the value and key do not need to match, and at any time you can replace the value object with a new object of any type.

NOTE: Be aware that the keys in the dictionary are case sensitive. For example, Name and name would represent two completely distinct keys in the dictionary.

```python
numbers = ('1','2','3','4','5','6','7','8','9','0')
letters = ('a','b','c','d','e','f')
punct = ('.', '!', '?')
charSetDict = {numbers:[], letters:[], punct:[]}

def display_cset (cset):
    print
    for x in cset.items():
        if x[0] == numbers:
            print "Numbers:"
        elif x[0] == letters:
            print "Letters:"
        elif x[0] == punct:
            print "Puctuation:"
        else:
            print "Unknown:"
        print x[1]


#Add new values to keys
cSet = raw_input("Insert characters: ")
for c in cSet:
    for x in charSetDict.keys():
        if c in x:
            charSetDict[x].append(c)
            break;

display_cset(charSetDict)


#Add new key and value
charSetDict["Special"] = ['%', '$', '#']
display_cset(charSetDict)

#Change value for existing key
charSetDict["Special"] = '><'
display_cset(charSetDict)
```

add_dict.py

```
Insert characters: abc 123 .
Numbers:
['1', '2', '3']
Puctuation:
['.']
Letters:
['a', 'b', 'c']

Numbers:
['1', '2', '3']
Puctuation:
['.']
Letters:
['a', 'b', 'c']
Unknown:
['%', '$', '#']

Numbers:
['1', '2', '3']
Puctuation:
['.']
Letters:
['a', 'b', 'c']
Unknown:
><
```

Output of add_dict.py

Retrieving a Value from a Dictionary

```
validkeys = (1,2,3)
keyGenDict={'keys':[1,2,3],1:'blue',2:'fast',
            3:'test','key':2}

print keyGenDict.keys()
print keyGenDict.values()
```

```
print keyGenDict.items()
val = keyGenDict["key"]
keyGenDict["key"] = 1
val = keyGenDict["key"]
```

A value can be retrieved from a dictionary using several different methods. The most common is to access the value directly by specifying the associated key in square brackets following the dictionary variable.

A list of values contained in a dictionary can be retrieved using the values() method. The values method returns a list containing all objects that are values in the dictionary.

Similarly, you can obtain just a list of keys using the keys() method. The keys method returns a list of objects that are currently being used as keys in the dictionary. The list of keys is useful in many ways, such as creating a tuple of the keys for faster lookups in the dictionary.

You can also get a list of key and value pairs by using the items() method. The items method returns a list that contains two-element tuples of each key and value pair in the dictionary.

```
validkeys = (1,2,3)
keyGenDict={'keys':[1,2,3],1:'blue',2:'fast',
            3:'test','key':2}

def show_key (key):
    if(key in validkeys):
        keyVal = (keyGenDict["keys"])[key-1]
        print "Key = " + keyGenDict[keyVal]
    else:
        print("Invalid key")

#Retrieving dictionary key list
```

```
print keyGenDict.keys()

#Retrieving dictionary value list
print keyGenDict.values()

#Retrieving dictionary key and value list
print keyGenDict.items()

#Retrieve value from key
val = keyGenDict["key"]
show_key(val)

keyGenDict["key"] = 1
val = keyGenDict["key"]
show_key(val)
```

ret_dict.py

```
['keys', 1, 2, 3, 'key']
[[1, 2, 3], 'blue', 'fast', 'test', 2]
[('keys', [1, 2, 3]), (1, 'blue'), (2, 'fast'),
 (3, 'test'), ('key', 2)]
Key = fast
Key = blue
```

Output of ret_dict.py

Slicing a Dictionary

```
year = {1:'January', 2:'February', 3:'March',
4:'April',\
        5:'May', 6:'June', 7:'July', 8:'August',\
        9:'September', 10:'October', 11:'November',\
        12:'December'}

months = year.keys()
months.sort()
```

```
halfCount = len(months)/2
half = months[0:halfCount]
firstHalf = {}
for x in half:
        firstHalf[x] = year[x]
```

There is no specific method to get a slice of a dictionary; however, this will be a common task that deserves some attention. The best way to slice out a subset of a dictionary is to first get the list of keys using the keys method. From the full list of keys, create a subset of that list through *slicing* or whatever means are necessary.

Once you have a specific subset of keys in the directory, you can pull out the values from the original dictionary and add them to a new dictionary.

If you want to keep the original dictionary intact, use the get method to pull out the value. However, if you want the value and keys removed from the original dictionary, use the pop method.

```
year = {1:'January', 2:'February', 3:'March',
4:'April',\
        5:'May', 6:'June', 7:'July', 8:'August',\
        9:'September', 10:'October', 11:'November',\
        12:'December'}

print year

#Get list of keys
months = year.keys()

#Create subset of keys
months.sort()
halfCount = len(months)/2
half = months[0:halfCount]

#Create new dictionary from subset of keys
```

```
firstHalf = {}
for x in half:
        firstHalf[x] = year[x]

print firstHalf
```

sub_dict.py

```
{1: 'January', 2: 'February', 3: 'March', 4:
'April', 5: 'May', 6: 'June', 7: 'July',
8: 'August', 9: 'September', 10: 'October',
11: 'November', 12: 'December'}

{1: 'January', 2: 'February', 3: 'March',
4: 'April', 5: 'May', 6: 'June'}
```

Output of sub_dict.py

Swapping Keys for Values in a Dictionary

```
myDictionary = {'color':'blue', 'speed':'fast',
 'number':1, 5:'number'}
swapDictionary = {}
for key, val in myDictionary.iteritems():
    swapDictionary[val] = key
```

Currently, there is not a method in Python to swap around the keys and values. However, this can be very useful if you are using a dictionary in which you may frequently need to look up items by value. Rather than searching through the entire dictionary each time, you could create an alternative dictionary that has the values swapped.

To swap the keys and values in a dictionary, simply iterate through the items in the dictionary using the iteritems method and use the values as keys assigning the original key as the value.

NOTE: The values must be of legal key types for the keys and values to be swapped.

```
myDictionary = {'color':'blue', 'speed':'fast',
 'number':1, 5:'number'}

print myDictionary

#Swap keys for values
swapDictionary = {}
for key, val in myDictionary.iteritems():
    swapDictionary[val] = key

print swapDictionary
```

swap_dict.py

```
{'color': 'blue', 'speed': 'fast',
 'number': 1, 5: 'number'}
{'blue': 'color', 1: 'number',
 'number': 5, 'fast': 'speed'}
```

Output of swap_dict.py

4

Managing Files

As with any well-developed scripting language, Python is very prepared to handle the need to directly manage and manipulate files. Python includes several built-in functions, as well as additional modules to help manage files. These functions and modules provide the versatility and power to handle file parsing, data storage and retrieval, and filesystem management, as well as archive management.

It's not possible to adequately address all the file management features of Python in this book; however, this chapter will provide the most common phrases to create and use files, manage files on a file system, and archive files for storage or distribution.

Opening and Closing Files

```
file = open(inPath, 'rU')
file = open(outPath, 'wb')
file.close()
```

To use most of the built-in file functions in Python, you will need to first open the file, perform whatever file operations are necessary, and then close it. Python uses the simple open(*path* [,*mode* [,*buffersize*]]) call to open files for both reading and writing. The *path* is a path string pointing to the file. The *mode* determines what mode the file will be opened in, as shown in Table 4.1.

Table 4.1   **File Modes for Python's Built-In File Functions**

Mode	Description
r	Opens an existing file for reading.
w	Opens a file for writing. If the file already exists, the contents are deleted. If the file does not already exist, a new one is created.
a	Opens an existing file for updating, keeping the existing contents intact.
r+	Opens a file for both reading and writing. The existing contents are kept intact.
w+	Opens a file for both writing and reading. The existing contents are deleted.
a+	Opens a file for both reading and writing. The existing contents are kept intact.
b	Is applied in addition to one of the read, write, or append modes. Opens the file in binary mode.
U	Is applied in addition to one of the read, write, or append modes. Applies the "universal" new-line translator to the file as it is opened.

The optional *buffersize* argument specifies which buffering mode should be used when accessing the file. 0 indicates that the file should be unbuffered, 1 indicates line-buffering, and any other positive number indicates a specific buffer size to be used when accessing the file. Buffering the file improves performance because part of the file is cached in computer memory.

Omitting this argument or specifying a negative number results in the system default buffer size to be used.

After using the file, you should close it using the built-in `close()` function. This will free up the system resources and keep the file from being held open any longer than necessary.

NOTE: Using the universal newline mode U is extremely useful if you need to deal with files that are created by applications that are not consistent in managing newline characters. The universal newline mode converts all the different variations (\r, \n, \r\n) to the standard \n character.

```python
inPath = "input.txt"
outPath = "output.txt"

#Open a file for reading
file = open(inPath, 'rU')
if file:
    # read from file here (see Reading an Entire
File
    # later in this chapter for more info)
    file.close()
else:
    print "Error Opening File."

#Open a file for writing
file = open(outPath, 'wb')
if file:
    # write to file here (see Writing a File later
    # in this chapter for more info)
    file.close()
else:
    print "Error Opening File."
```

open_file.py

Reading an Entire File

```
buffer += open(filePath, 'rU').read()
inList = open(filePath, 'rU').readlines()
while(1):
    bytes = file.read(5)
    if bytes:
        buffer += bytes
```

Python provides several methods to read the entire contents of a file. The first is to open the file and call the read() function. This reads the entire contents of the file until an EOF marker is encountered and returns the contents of the file as a string.

Another method to read an entire file is to use the readlines() function. This reads the entire contents of the file, separating each line into individual strings, until an EOF marker is encountered. Once the end of the file is found, a list of strings representing each line is returned.

In case of very large files, you might want to read only a specific number of bytes at a time. Use the read(*bytes*) function to read a specific number of bytes at a time, which can then be processed more easily. This will read a specific number of bytes from the file if possible and return them as a string. If the first character read is an EOF marker, null is returned.

The code in read_file.py demonstrates how to read the entire contents at once, one line at a time, as well as a specific number of bytes from a file.

```
filePath = "input.txt"

#Read entire file into a buffer
buffer = "Read buffer:\n"
```

```
buffer += open(filePath, 'rU').read()
print buffer

#Read lines into a buffer
buffer = "Readline buffer:\n"
inList = open(filePath, 'rU').readlines()
print inList
for line in inList:
    buffer += line
print buffer

#Read bytes into a buffer
buffer = "Read buffer:\n"
file = open(filePath, 'rU')
while(1):
    bytes = file.read(5)
    if bytes:
        buffer += bytes
    else:
        break

print buffer
```

read_file.py

```
Read buffer:
Line 1
Line 2
Line 3
Line 4

['Line 1\n', 'Line 2\n', 'Line 3\n', 'Line 4\n']
Readline buffer:
Line 1
Line 2
Line 3
```

```
Line 4

Read buffer:
Line 1
Line 2
Line 3
Line 4
```

Output from read_file py code

Reading a Single Line from a File

```
print linecache.getline(filePath, 1)
print linecache.getline(filePath, 3)
linecache.clearcache()
```

The linecache module in Python is an extremely useful tool if you need to access specific lines in certain files multiple times. The linecache module caches the lines in a file in memory the first time they are read. Although this does not provide any advantage the first time the file is accessed, it does speed up consecutive accesses immensely.

The getline(*filename, lineno*) function of the linecache module accepts a filename and line number as its arguments. It then reads the line from the file, caches it in memory for later use, and then returns a string representation of the line. The clearcache() function of the linecache module frees up the cache memory by removing all lines that have been previously read.

```
import linecache
filePath = "input.txt"

print linecache.getline(filePath, 1)
print linecache.getline(filePath, 3)
linecache.clearcache()
```

line_cache.py

```
Line 1

Line 3
```

Output from line_cache.py code

Accessing Each Word in a File

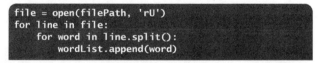

A useful tool when processing files is to separate each word in the file and process them one at a time. The words can be individually processed by opening the file, reading each line into a string, and then splitting the strings into words using the split() function.

The program read_words.py shows a simple example of reading a file and processing the words one at time. The lines in the file are processed one at a time using a for loop. The split() function splits the line into a list of words based on spaces because no other character was passed as the separator argument. Once the words are separated, they can be individually processed into lists, dictionaries, and so on.

```
filePath = "input.txt"
wordList = []
wordCount = 0

#Read lines into a list
file = open(filePath, 'rU')
for line in file:
    for word in line.split():
        wordList.append(word)
        wordCount += 1
print wordList
print "Total words = %d" % wordCount
```

read_words.py

```
['Line', '1', 'Line', '2', 'Line', '3', 'Line', '4']
Total words = 8
```

Output from read_words.py code

Writing a File

```
file.writelines(wordList)
file.write("\n\nFormatted text:\n")
print >>file,"\t%s Color Adjust" % word
```

Just as with reading the contents of a file, there are several ways to write data out to a file. The easiest, yet the most dynamic and powerful, is the write(*string*) function. The write function writes the *string* argument to the file at the current file pointer. Although the write function itself is relatively simple, the power of Python with regard to string manipulation makes the capabilities of the write function virtually limitless.

Python provides the writelines(*sequence*) function to save time writing a list of data out to the file. The `writelines` function typically accepts a list of strings and writes those strings to the file.

Another option available in Python is to redirect the `print` statement out to a file using the `>>` redirection operation. This allows you to use the versatility of the Python `print` function to format and write data out to a file.

```python
wordList = ["Red", "Blue", "Green"]
filePath = "output.txt"

#Write a list to a file
file = open(filePath, 'wU')
file.writelines(wordList)

#Write a string to a file
file.write("\n\nFormatted text:\n")

#Print directly to a file
for word in wordList:
    print >>file,"\t%s Color Adjust" % word

file.close()
```

write_file.py

```
RedBlueGreen

Formatted text:
        Red Color Adjust
        Blue Color Adjust
        Green Color Adjust
```

Contents of output.txt file

Determining the Number of Lines in a File

```
lineCount = len(open(filePath, 'rU').readlines())
print "File %s has %d lines." % (filePath,
lineCount)
```

When parsing files using Python, it's useful to know exactly how many lines are contained in the file. The example in file_lines.py shows a simple method to determine the number of lines contained in a file by first opening it, using readlines() to generate a list of lines, and then using the len() function to determine the number of lines in the list.

NOTE: For large files, using readlines() to generate a list lines in a file might be impractical because of the amount of memory and processing time necessary.

```
filePath = "input.txt"

lineCount = len(open(filePath, 'rU').readlines())
print "File %s has %d lines." % (filePath,
lineCount)
```

file_lines.py

```
File input.txt has 4 lines.
```

Output from file_lines.py code

Walking the Directory Tree

```
tree = os.walk(path)
for directory in tree:
    printDirectory(directory)
```

Python provides a powerful directory tree-walking function in the os module. The walk(*path*) function will walk the directory tree, and for each directory in the tree create a three-tuple containing (1) the dirpath, (2) a list of dirnames, and (3) a list of filenames.

Once the tuples have been created, they can be processed one at a time as elements of a list. For each tuple, you can access the path to the directory represented directly by using the 0 index into the tuple. Lists of the subdirectories and files contained in the directory can likewise be accessed using the 1 and 2 indexes, respectively.

The example in dir_tree.py shows how to use the os.walk(path) function to walk a directory tree and print out a formatted listing of the tree.

```
import os
path = "/books/python"

def printFiles(dirList, spaceCount):
    for file in dirList:
        print "/".rjust(spaceCount+1) + file

def printDirectory(dirEntry):
    print dirEntry[0] + "/"
    printFiles(dirEntry[2], len(dirEntry[0]))

tree = os.walk(path)
for directory in tree:
    printDirectory(directory)
```

dir_tree.py

```
/books/python/
              /Python Proposal.doc
              /Python_Phrasebook_TOC.doc
              /python_schedule.xls
              /template.doc
              /TOC_Notes.doc
/books/python\CH2/
                  /ch2.doc
/books/python\CH2\code/
                       /comp_str.py
                       /end_str.py
                       /eval_str.py
                       /format_str.py
                       /join_str.py
                       /output.txt
                       /replace_str.py
                       /search_str.py
                       /split_str.py
                       /trim_str.py
                       /unicode_str.py
                       /var_str.py
/books/python\CH3/
                  /ch3.doc
```

Output from dir_tree.py code

Renaming Files

```
os.remove(newFileName)
os.rename(oldFileName, newFileName)
```

A common task when parsing files using Python is to either delete the file or at least rename it once the data has been processed. The easiest way to accomplish this is to use the os.remove(*newFile*) and os.rename(*oldFile*, *newFile*) function in the os module.

The example in ren_file shows how to rename a file by first detecting whether the new filename already exists and then removing the existing file. Once the existing file has been removed, the rename function can be used to rename the file.

```python
import os

oldFileName = "/books/python/CH4/code/output.txt"
newFileName = "/books/python/CH4/code/output.old"

#Old Listing
for file in os.listdir("/books/python/CH4/code/"):
    if file.startswith("output"):
        print file

#Remove file if the new name already exists
if os.access(newFileName, os.X_OK):
    print "Removing " + newFileName
    os.remove(newFileName)

#Rename the file
os.rename(oldFileName, newFileName)

#New Listing
for file in os.listdir("/books/python/CH4/code/"):
    if file.startswith("output"):
        print file
```

ren_file.py

```
output.old
output.txt
Removing /books/python/CH4/code/output.old
output.old
```

Output from ren_file.py code

Recursively Deleting Files and Subdirectories

```
for file in dirList:
    os.remove(dirPath + "/" + file)
for dir in emptyDirs:
    os.rmdir(dir)
```

To recursively delete files and subdirectories in Python, use the walk(path) function in the os module. For a more detailed description of the walk function, refer to the "Walking the Directory Tree" section earlier in this chapter.

The walk function will automatically create a list of tuples representing the directories that need to be deleted. To recursively delete a tree, walk through the list of directories and delete each file contained in the files list (third item in the tuple).

The trick is removing the directories. Because a directory cannot be removed until it is completely empty, the files must first be deleted and then the directories must be removed in reverse order, starting with the deepest subdirectory.

The example in del_tree.py shows how to use the os.walk(path) function to walk a directory tree and delete the files, and then recursively remove the subdirectories.

```
import os

emptyDirs = []
path = "/trash/deleted_files"

def deleteFiles(dirList, dirPath):
```

```
    for file in dirList:
        print "Deleting " + file
        os.remove(dirPath + "/" + file)

def removeDirectory(dirEntry):
    print "Deleting files in " + dirEntry[0]
    deleteFiles(dirEntry[2], dirEntry[0])
    emptyDirs.insert(0, dirEntry[0])

#Enumerate the entries in the tree
tree = os.walk(path)
for directory in tree:
    removeDirectory(directory)

#Remove the empty directories
for dir in emptyDirs:
    print "Removing " + dir
    os.rmdir(dir)
```

del_tree.py

```
Deleting files in /trash/deleted_files
Deleting 102.ini
Deleting 103.ini
Deleting 104.ini
Deleting 105.ini
Deleting 106.ini
Deleting 107.ini
Deleting 108.ini
Deleting 109.ini
Deleting files in /trash/deleted_files\Test
Deleting 111.ini
Deleting 114.ini
Deleting 115.ini
Deleting files in /trash/deleted_files\Test\Test2
Deleting 112.ini
Deleting 113.ini
```

```
Removing /trash/deleted_files\Test\Test2
Removing /trash/deleted_files\Test
Removing /trash/deleted_files
```

Output from del_tree.py code

Searching for Files Based on Extension

```
for ext in pattern.split(";"):
    extList.append(ext.lstrip("*"))
....
if file.endswith(ext):
    print "/".rjust(spaceCount+1) + file
```

One of the most common file functions is to search for files based on extension. The example in find_file.py shows one way to search for files based on a string of extensions. The search is handled by first creating a list of the file extensions by splitting the pattern string using the split() function.

Once the list of extensions is created, walk the directory tree and check to see whether the file's extension matches one in the list by using the endswith(*string*) function on the file.

```
import os
path = "/books/python"
pattern = "*.py;*.doc"

#Print files that match to file extensions
def printFiles(dirList, spaceCount, typeList):
    for file in dirList:
        for ext in typeList:
```

```python
            if file.endswith(ext):
                print "/".rjust(spaceCount+1) + file
                break

#Print each sub-directory
def printDirectory(dirEntry, typeList):
    print dirEntry[0] + "/"
    printFiles(dirEntry[2], len(dirEntry[0]),
typeList)

#Convert pattern string to list of file extensions
extList = []
for ext in pattern.split(";"):
    extList.append(ext.lstrip("*"))

#Walk the tree to print files
for directory in os.walk(path):
    printDirectory(directory, extList)
```

find_file.py

```
/books/python/
              /Python Proposal.doc
              /Python_Phrasebook_TOC.doc
              /template.doc
              /TOC_Notes.doc
/books/python\CH2/
                  /ch2.doc
/books/python\CH2\code/
                       /comp_str.py
                       /end_str.py
                       /eval_str.py
                       /format_str.py
                       /join_str.py
                       /replace_str.py
                       /search_str.py
                       /split_str.py
```

```
                              /trim_str.py
                              /unicode_str.py
                              /var_str.py
/books/python\CH3/
                    /ch3.doc
```

Output from find_file.py code

Creating a TAR File

```
tFile = tarfile.open("files.tar", 'w')
files = os.listdir(".")
for f in files:
    tFile.add(f)
```

The tarfile module, included with Python, provides a
set of easy-to-use methods to create and manipulate
TAR files. The open(*filename* [, *mode* [, *fileobj* [,
bufsize]]]) method must be called with the write
mode set to create a new TAR. Table 4.2 shows the
different modes available when opening a TAR file.

Once the TAR file has been opened in write mode,
files can be added to it using the add(*name* [,*arcname*
[, *recursive*]]) method. The add method adds the file
or directory specified in *name* to the archive. The
optional *arcname* argument enables you to specify what
name the file should have inside the archive. The
recursive argument accepts a Boolean true or false to
determine whether or not to recursively add the contents of directories to the archive.

Table 4.2   **File Modes for Python's tarfile Module**

Mode	Description
r	(Default) Opens a TAR file for reading. If the file is compressed, it will be decompressed.
r:	Opens a TAR file for reading with no compression.
w or w:	Opens a TAR file for writing with no compression.
a or a:	Opens a TAR file for appending with no compression.
r:gz	Opens a TAR file for reading with gzip compression.
w:gz	Opens a TAR file for writing with gzip compression.
r:bz2	Opens a TAR file for reading with bzip2 compression.
w:bz2	Opens a TAR file for writing with bzip2 compression.

NOTE: To open a TAR file for sequential access only, replace the : character in the mode with a | character. The append mode is not available for the sequential access option.

```
import os
import tarfile

#Create Tar file
```

```python
tFile = tarfile.open("files.tar", 'w')

#Add directory contents to tar file
files = os.listdir(".")
for f in files:
    tFile.add(f)

#List files in tar
for f in tFile.getnames():
    print "Added %s" % f

tFile.close()
```

tar_file.py

```
Added add_zip.py
Added del_tree.py
Added dir_tree.py
Added extract.txt
Added extract_tar.py
Added file_lines.py
Added find_file.py
Added get_zip.py
Added input.txt
Added open_file.py
Added output.old
Added read_file.py
Added read_line.py
Added read_words.py
Added ren_file.py
Added tar_file.py
Added write_file.py
```

Output from tar_file.py code

Extracting a File from a TAR File

```
tFile = tarfile.open("files.tar", 'r')
tFile.extract(f, extractPath)
```

The tarfile module includes the extract(*file* [, *path*]) method to extract files specified by the *file* argument and place them in the location specified by the *path* argument. If no path is specified, the current working directory becomes the destination.

The example in extract_tar.py opens the TAR file created in the previous phrase and extracts only the Python files to a directory called /bin/py.

```
import os
import tarfile

extractPath = "/bin/py"

#Open Tar file
tFile = tarfile.open("files.tar", 'r')

#Extract py files in tar
for f in tFile.getnames():
    if f.endswith("py"):
        print "Extracting %s" % f
        tFile.extract(f, extractPath)
    else:
        print "%s is not a Python file." % f

tFile.close()
```

extract_tar.py

```
Extracting add_zip.py
Extracting del_tree.py
Extracting dir_tree.py
extract.txt is not a Python file.
Extracting extract_tar.py
Extracting file_lines.py
Extracting find_file.py
Extracting get_zip.py
input.txt is not a Python file.
Extracting open_file.py
output.old is not a Python file.
Extracting read_file.py
Extracting read_line.py
Extracting read_words.py
Extracting ren_file.py
Extracting tar_file.py
Extracting write_file.py
```

Output from extract_tar.py code

Adding Files to a ZIP File

```
tFile = zipfile.ZipFile("files.zip", 'w')
files = os.listdir(".")
for f in files:
    tFile.write(f)
```

The zipfile module, included with Python, provides a set of easy-to-use methods to create and manipulate ZIP files. The ZipFile(*filename* [, *mode* [, *compression*]]) method creates or opens a ZIP file depending on the mode specified. The available modes for ZIP files are r, w, and a to read, write, or append, respectively. Using the w mode will create a new ZIP file or truncate the existing file to zero if it already exists.

The optional *compression* argument will accept either the ZIP_STORED(not compressed) or ZIP_DEFLATED(compressed) compression options to set the default compression when writing files to the archive.

Once the ZIP file has been opened in write mode, files can be added to it using the write(*filename* [,*arcname* [, *compression*]]) method. The write method adds the file specified in *filename* to the archive. The optional *arcname* argument enables you to specify what name the file should have inside the archive.

```
import os
import zipfile

#Create the zip file
tFile = zipfile.ZipFile("files.zip", 'w')

#Write directory contents to the zip file
files = os.listdir(".")
for f in files:
    tFile.write(f)

#List archived files
for f in tFile.namelist():
    print "Added %s" % f


tFile.close()
```

add_zip.py

```
Added add_zip.py
Added del_tree.py
Added dir_tree.py
Added extract.txt
Added extract_tar.py
```

```
Added files.zip
Added file_lines.py
Added find_file.py
Added get_zip.py
Added input.txt
Added open_file.py
Added output.old
Added read_file.py
Added read_line.py
Added read_words.py
Added ren_file.py
Added tar_file.py
Added write_file.py
```

Output from add_zip.py code

Retrieving Files from a ZIP File

```
tFile = zipfile.ZipFile("files.zip", 'r')
buffer = tFile.read("ren_file.py")
```

Retrieving file contents from a ZIP file is easily done using the read(*filename*) method included in the zip-file module. Once the ZIP file is opened in read mode, the read method is called and the contents of the specified file are returned as a string. Once the contents are returned, they can be added to a list or dictionary, printed to the screen, written to a file, or any number of other possibilities.

The example in get_zip.py opens the ZIP file created in the previous phrase, reads the Python file ren_file.py, prints the contents to the screen, and then writes the contents to a new file called extract.txt.

```
import os
import zipfile


tFile = zipfile.ZipFile("files.zip", 'r')

#List info for archived file
print tFile.getinfo("input.txt")

#Read zipped file into a buffer
buffer = tFile.read("ren_file.py")
print buffer

#Write zipped file contents to new file
f = open("extract.txt", "w")
f.write(buffer)
f.close()

tFile.close()
```

get_zip.py

```
<zipfile.ZipInfo instance at 0x008DCB70>
import os

oldFileName = "/books/python/CH4/code/output.txt"
newFileName = "/books/python/CH4/code/output.old"

#Old Listing
for file in os.listdir("/books/python/CH4/code/"):
    if file.startswith("output"):
        print file

#Remove file if the new name already exists
if os.access(newFileName, os.X_OK):
    print "Removing " + newFileName
```

```
    os.remove(newFileName)

#Rename the file
os.rename(oldFileName, newFileName)

#New Listing
for file in os.listdir("/books/python/CH4/code/"):
    if file.startswith("output"):
        print file
```

Output from get_zip.py code

5

Managing Threads

The Python language provides several functions and modules that will allow you to create, start, and control multiple threads. This chapter is designed to help you understand how to quickly implement threads into your programs to provide faster and easier processing of data.

Working with multiple threads that share the same data at the same time can be problematic. For example, two or more threads could try to access the same data at the same time, causing race conditions that can lead to deadlocks. For that reason, this chapter includes using thread locks and queues to manage data so that access to the CPU and data can be synchronized across multiple threads.

Timer-interrupted threads can be extremely valuable to provide notification status, as well as to clean up operations at specific intervals. The final phrase of this chapter discusses how to create and start a timer-interrupted thread.

CAUTION: You should be careful when using multiple threads that invoke methods in some of the extension modules. Not all the extension modules are particularly friendly. For example, they might block execution of all other threads for extended amounts of time until they are completed. However, most functions included in the Python standard library are written to work well in a multithreaded environment.

Starting a New Thread

```
thread.start_new_thread(print_time, ("Thread01",
2,))
thread.start_new_thread(print_time, ("Thread02",
4,))
```

The start_new_thread(*function*, *args* [, *kwargs*]) method in the Python thread module enables a fast and efficient way to create new threads in both Linux and Windows. It accepts a function name as the first parameter and a set of arguments as the second. The optional third parameter allows you to pass a dictionary containing keyword arguments.

The start_new_thread method creates a new thread and then starts code execution of the function. Control is immediately returned to the calling thread, and the new thread executes the specified function and returns silently.

NOTE: If the code being executed by a new thread encounters an exception, a stack trace will be printed and the thread will exit. However, other threads will continue to run.

Although it is very effective for low-level threading, the thread module is very limited compared to the newer threading module.

```
import thread
import time

def print_time(threadName, delay):
    while 1:
        time.sleep(delay)
        print "%s: %s" % (threadName, \
            time.ctime(time.time()))

#Start threads to print time at different intervals
thread.start_new_thread(print_time, ("Thread01",
2,))
thread.start_new_thread(print_time, ("Thread02",
4,))

while 1:
    pass
```

create_thread.py

```
Thread01: Wed Jun 14 12:46:21 2006
Thread01: Wed Jun 14 12:46:23 2006
Thread02: Wed Jun 14 12:46:23 2006
Thread01: Wed Jun 14 12:46:25 2006
Thread01: Wed Jun 14 12:46:27 2006
Thread02: Wed Jun 14 12:46:27 2006
Thread01: Wed Jun 14 12:46:29 2006
Thread01: Wed Jun 14 12:46:31 2006
. . . . .
```

Output from create_thread.py code

Creating and Exiting Threads

```
class newThread (threading.Thread):
    def __init__(self, threadID, name, counter):
        self.threadID = threadID
        self.name = name
        self.counter = counter
        threading.Thread.__init__(self)
. . . . .
if doExit:
    thread.exit()
```

The newer threading module included with Python 2.4 provides much more powerful, high-level support for threads than the thread module discussed in the previous phrase. It is a little more complicated to implement; however, it provides the ability to better control and synchronize threads.

The threading module introduces a Thread class that represents a separate thread of execution. To implement a new thread using the threading module, first define a new subclass of the Thread class. Override the __init__(self [,*args*]) method to add additional arguments. Then override the run(self [,*args*]) method to implement what the thread should do when started.

Once you have created the new Thread subclass, you can create an instance of it and then start a new thread by invoking the start() or run() methods.

```
import threading
import thread
import time

doExit = 0

class newThread (threading.Thread):
```

```python
    def __init__(self, threadID, name, counter):
        self.threadID = threadID
        self.name = name
        self.counter = counter
        threading.Thread.__init__(self)
    def run(self):
        print "Starting " + self.name
        print_time(self.name, self.counter, 5)
        print "Exiting " + self.name

def print_time(threadName, delay, counter):
    while counter:
        if doExit:
            thread.exit()
        time.sleep(delay)
        print "%s: %s" % (threadName, \
            time.ctime(time.time()))
        counter -= 1

#Create new threads
thread1 = newThread(1, "Thread01", 1)
thread2 = newThread(2, "Thread02", 2)

#Start new Threads
thread1.start()
thread2.run()


while thread2.isAlive():
    if not thread1.isAlive():
        doExit = 1

    pass

print "Exiting Main Thread"
```

exit_thread.py

```
Starting Thread01
Starting Thread02
Thread01: Wed Jun 14 13:06:10 2006
Thread01: Wed Jun 14 13:06:11 2006
Thread02: Wed Jun 14 13:06:11 2006
Thread01: Wed Jun 14 13:06:12 2006
Thread01: Wed Jun 14 13:06:13 2006
Thread02: Wed Jun 14 13:06:13 2006
Thread01: Wed Jun 14 13:06:14 2006
Exiting Thread01
Thread02: Wed Jun 14 13:06:15 2006
Exiting Main Thread
```

Output from exit_thread.py code

Synchronizing Threads

```
threadLock = threading.Lock()
. . .
threadLock.acquire()
print_time(self.name, self.counter, 3)
threadLock.release()
```

The threading module provided with Python includes a simple-to-implement locking mechanism that will allow you to synchronize threads. A new lock is created by calling the Lock() method, which returns the new lock.

Once the new lock object has been created, you can force threads to run synchronously by calling the acquire(*blocking*) method. The optional *blocking* parameter enables you to control whether the thread will wait to acquire the lock. If blocking is set to 0, the thread will return immediately with a 0 value if the lock cannot be acquired and with a 1 if the lock was acquired. If blocking is set to 1, the thread will block and wait for the lock to be released.

When you are finished with the lock, the lock is released by calling the release() method of the new lock object.

```
import threading
import time

class newThread (threading.Thread):
    def __init__(self, threadID, name, counter):
        self.threadID = threadID
        self.name = name
        self.counter = counter
        threading.Thread.__init__(self)
    def run(self):
        print "Starting " + self.name
#Get lock to synchronize threads
        threadLock.acquire()
        print_time(self.name, self.counter, 3)
#Free lock to release next thread
        threadLock.release()

def print_time(threadName, delay, counter):
    while counter:
        time.sleep(delay)
        print "%s: %s" % (threadName, \
            time.ctime(time.time()))
        counter -= 1

threadLock = threading.Lock()
threads = []

#Create new threads
thread1 = newThread(1, "Thread01", 1)
thread2 = newThread(2, "Thread02", 2)

#Start new Threads
thread1.start()
```

```
thread2.start()

#Add threads to thread list
threads.append(thread1)
threads.append(thread2)

#Wait for all threads to complete
for t in threads:
    t.join()

print "Exiting Main Thread"
```

sync_thread.py

```
Starting Thread01
Starting Thread02
Thread01: Tue Jun 20 10:06:24 2006
Thread01: Tue Jun 20 10:06:25 2006
Thread01: Tue Jun 20 10:06:26 2006
Thread02: Tue Jun 20 10:06:28 2006
Thread02: Tue Jun 20 10:06:30 2006
Thread02: Tue Jun 20 10:06:32 2006
Exiting Main Thread
```

Output from sync_thread.py code

Implementing a Multithreaded Priority Queue

```
queueLock = threading.Lock()
workQueue = Queue.Queue(10)
queueLock.acquire()
for word in wordList:
    workQueue.put(word)
queueLock.release()
while not workQueue.empty():
```

```
    pass
. . .
queueLock.acquire()
if not workQueue.empty():
    data = q.get()
    queueLock.release()
```

The Queue module provides an invaluable way to manage processing large amounts of data on multiple threads. The Queue module allows you to create a new queue object that can hold a specific number of items. Items can be added and removed from the queue using the get() and put() methods of the queue object.

The queue object also includes the empty(), full(), and qsize() methods to determine whether the queue is empty, full, or the approximate size, respectively. The qsize method is not always reliable because of multiple threads removing items from the queue.

If necessary, you can implement the thread locking discussed in the previous phrase to control access to the queue. This will make queue management much safer and provide you with more control of the data processing.

```
import Queue
import threading
import time
import thread

doExit = 0

class newThread (threading.Thread):
    def __init__(self, threadID, name, q):
        self.threadID = threadID
        self.name = name
        self.q = q
        threading.Thread.__init__(self)
```

```python
    def run(self):
        print "Starting " + self.name
        process_data(self.name, self.q)
        print "Exiting " + self.name

def process_data(tName, q):
    while not doExit:
        queueLock.acquire()
        if not workQueue.empty():
            data = q.get()
            queueLock.release()
            print "%s processing %s" % (tName, data)
        else:
            queueLock.release()
        time.sleep(1)

threadList = ["Thread1", "Thread2", "Thread3"]
wordList = ["One", "Two", "Three", "Four", "Five"]
queueLock = threading.Lock()
workQueue = Queue.Queue(10)
threads = []
tID = 1

#Create new threads
for tName in threadList:
    thread = newThread(tID, tName, workQueue)
    thread.start()
    threads.append(thread)
    tID += 1

#Fill the queue
queueLock.acquire()
for word in wordList:
    workQueue.put(word)
queueLock.release()

#Wait for queue to empty
while not workQueue.empty():
```

```
    pass

#Notify threads it's time to exit
doExit = 1

#Wait for all threads to complete
for t in threads:
    t.join()

print "Exiting Main Thread"
```

queue_thread.py

```
Starting Thread1
Starting Thread2
Starting Thread3
Thread1 processing One
Thread2 processing Two
Thread3 processing Three
Thread1 processing Four
Thread2 processing Five
Exiting Thread1
Exiting Thread2
Exiting Thread3
Exiting Main Thread
```

Output from queue_thread.py code

Initiating a Timer-Interrupted Thread

```
wakeCall = threading.Timer(waitTime, \
                clean_queue, (qPath ,))
wakeCall.start()
```

Common threads invoked on Linux servers are the timer threads to clean up resources, provide notification, and check status, as well as many other functions. The threading module included with Python provides an easy way of creating a simple timer-interrupted thread.

The Timer(*interval*, *func* [,*args* [, *kwargs*]]) method of the threading module creates a new timer-interrupted thread object. The *interval* specifies the number of seconds to wait before executing the function specified in the *func* argument.

Once the new timer-interrupted thread object is created, it can be started at any time using the start method of the object. Once the start method is invoked, the thread will wait the specified timer interval and then begin execution.

NOTE: A timer thread can be cancelled after it is started, using the cancel() method of the object, provided that the function has not yet been executed.

```python
import threading
import os

def clean_queue (qPath):
    jobList = os.listdir(qPath)
    for j in jobList:
        delPath = "%s/%s" % (qPath, j)
        os.remove(delPath)
        print "Removing " + delPath

qPath = "/print/queue01"
waitTime = 600 #10 minutes
```

```
#Create timer thread
wakeCall = threading.Timer(waitTime, \
                clean_queue, (qPath ,))

#Start timer thread
wakeCall.start()
```

timer_thread.py

```
Removing /print/queue01/102.txt
Removing /print/queue01/103.txt
Removing /print/queue01/104.txt
Removing /print/queue01/105.txt
Removing /print/queue01/106.txt
Removing /print/queue01/107.txt
```

Output from timer_thread.py code

6

Managing Databases

The ability to store data in a manageable database dramatically increases the options regarding the types of applications that can be created by Python. The Python language has built-in modules, as well as add-on modules, that provide an extensive platform for the persistent storage of data in various database formats.

This chapter familiarizes you with phrases used to create generic DBM files for simple persistent storage of data, as well as some advanced concepts such as pickling data to files and shelves. Most basic database needs can be handled by the DBM, pickle, and shelve modules. The advantage of those modules is that they do not require a backend database server.

This chapter also covers connecting to and using a MySQL server as the backend database engine for persistent storage. MySQLdb, available at http://www.mysql.org/, is an add-on Python package that conforms to the Python DB-API 2.0 specification. Python provides the DB-API specification to accommodate the numerous forms of SQL servers available. The specification provides the necessary framework to access most of the available SQL databases via add-on modules such as MySQLdb.

There are other SQL modules available for other SQL servers such as Oracle, JDBC, Sybase, and DB2, as well as others. Thanks to the Python DB-API spec, the phrases listed for MySQL can be used to access those SQL databases as well. You simply need to install the appropriate module and use that module's `connect` function to connect to the database.

NOTE: There might be some subtle differences among different database query strings, such as escape sequences.

Adding Entries to a DBM File

```
import anydbm
cityDB = anydbm.open("city.dbm", 'n')
for flight in flights:
    cityDB[flight] = cities[i]
cityDB.close()
```

The anydbm module provides a generic interface, allowing you to open databases based on several different lower-level packages that can be installed on the system. When imported, the anydbm module searches for the dbm, gdbm, and bsddb packages that provide access to the UNIX dbm, GNU DBM, and Berkely DB libraries, respectively. If none of those packages are available, the dumbdbm module is loaded to provide access to a simple DBM-style database library.

The adybdm module provides the open(*filename* [, *flag* [, *mode*]]) function that allows you to open and create databases (see the "Opening and Closing Files" phrase of Chapter 4, "Managing Files," for more details).

NOTE: When creating a new database, anydbm will try to use the database module that was first installed on the system.

The open function returns a database object that behaves much the same as a dictionary. Entries can be added to the database by assigning a value to a key using the d[*key*] = *value* syntax. The *key* must be a standard string, and the *value* must also be a standard string, except in the shelve module discussed in later phrases.

```python
import anydbm

cities = ["Dallas", "Los Angeles", "New York"]
flights = ["1144", "1045", "1520"]
times = ["230pm", "320pm", "420pm"]

#Create DBM file
cityDB = anydbm.open("city.dbm", 'n')
timeDB = anydbm.open("time.dbm", 'n')

#Add entries
i = 0
for flight in flights:
    cityDB[flight] = cities[i]
    i += 1
i = 0
for flight in flights:
    timeDB[flight] = times[i]
    i += 1

print cityDB.items()
print timeDB.items()

#Close DBM file
cityDB.close()
timeDB.close()
```

add_dbm.py

```
[('1144', 'Dallas'), ('1045', 'Los Angeles'),
 ('1520', 'New York')]
[('1144', '230pm'), ('1045', '320pm'),
 ('1520', '420pm')]
```

Output from add_dbm.py code

Retrieving Entries from a DBM File

```
import anydbm
cityDB = anydbm.open("city.dbm", 'r')
flights = cityDB.keys()
for flight in flights:
    print ("Flight %s arrives from %s at %s" %
(flight, cityDB[flight], timeDB[flight]))
    cityDB.close()
```

The anydbm module provides a generic interface allowing you to open databases based on several different lower-level packages that can be installed on the system. When imported, the anydbm module searches for the dbm, gdbm, or bsddb package. If none of those packages are available, the dumbdbm module is loaded and used for database I/O.

The anydbm module provides the open(*filename* [,*flag* [, *mode*]]) function that allows you to open and create databases (see the "Opening and Closing Files" phrase of Chapter 4 for more details).

NOTE: When opening an existing database, anydbm uses the whichdb module to determine which database module to use when opening the database.

Once the database has been opened, you can use the
database object similarly to a dictionary. You can use
the keys() and values() functions to retrieve a list of
keys or values, respectively. You can also access a specific value by referencing using the corresponding key.

```python
import anydbm

#Open DBM file for reading
cityDB = anydbm.open("city.dbm", 'r')
timeDB = anydbm.open("time.dbm", 'r')

#Get keys
flights = cityDB.keys()

#Use keys to get values
print "Arrivals"
print
"================================================"
for flight in flights:
    print ("Flight %s arrives from %s at %s" %
(flight, cityDB[flight], timeDB[flight]))

#Close DBM file
cityDB.close()
timeDB.close()
```

get_dbm.py

```
Arrivals
================================================
Flight 1144 arrives from Dallas at 230pm
Flight 1045 arrives from Los Angeles at 320pm
Flight 1520 arrives from New York at 420pm
```

Output from get_dbm.py code

Updating Entries in a DBM File

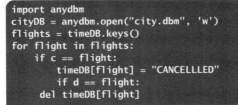

```
import anydbm
cityDB = anydbm.open("city.dbm", 'w')
flights = timeDB.keys()
for flight in flights:
    if c == flight:
        timeDB[flight] = "CANCELLLED"
        if d == flight:
      del timeDB[flight]
```

After the database has been opened, you can use the database object similarly to a dictionary. To change a value of an object in the database, assign a new value to the corresponding key using d[*key*] = *value*. To remove an object from the database, use del d[*key*] to reference the object by its specific key.

NOTE: The d.has_key(*key*) function can be extremely useful if you are not certain whether a specific key exists in the database.

```
import anydbm

flights = []
cancelled = ["1520", "1544"]
deleted = ["1144"]

def displayArrivals(header):
    print header
    print "========================================="
    for flight in flights:
        print ("Flight %s from %s arrives at %s" %
            (flight, cityDB[flight],
timeDB[flight]))

#Open DBM file for reading
```

```
cityDB = anydbm.open("city.dbm", 'w')
timeDB = anydbm.open("time.dbm", 'w')

#Get keys
flights = timeDB.keys()

#Display arrivals
displayArrivals("Arrivals")

#Update DBM
for flight in flights:
    for c in cancelled:
        if c == flight:
            timeDB[flight] = "CANCELLED"
            break
    for d in deleted:
        if d == flight:
            del timeDB[flight]
            del cityDB[flight]
            break

#Display updated arrivals
flights = timeDB.keys()
displayArrivals("Updated Arrivals")

#Close DBM file
cityDB.close()
timeDB.close()
```

update_dbm.py

```
Arrivals
================================================
Flight 1144 from Dallas arrives at 230pm
Flight 1045 from Los Angeles arrives at 320pm
Flight 1520 from New York arrives at 420pm

Updated Arrivals
```

```
=================================================
Flight 1045 from Los Angeles arrives at 320pm
Flight 1520 from New York arrives at CANCELLED
```

Output from update_dbm.py code

Pickling Objects to a File

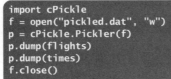

```
import cPickle
f = open("pickled.dat", "w")
p = cPickle.Pickler(f)
p.dump(flights)
p.dump(times)
f.close()
```

Pickling data to files is one of the simplest ways to get around the limitation that DBM files have of only allowing simple text string storage. The pickle and cPickle modules included with Python provide a simple-to-use interface to pickle entire objects to a file for persistent storage.

NOTE: The cPickler object is much faster than the pickler object; however, it will not allow you to subclass the pickler and unpickler objects for advanced handling of data.

The idea of pickling is to take an existing Python object and structure the data in such a way that it can be easily written out to an existing file and read back again.

The first step in pickling Python objects is to open a file with the write permission. Once the file has been opened, use the Pickler(*file*) method to create a pickler object. The Pickler method accepts a standard file object as its only parameter and returns the pickler object that is used to write objects to the file.

Once the pickler object has been created, you can use the dump(*object*) method to write almost any Python object to the file. The dump method pickles the object and writes it to the file. As the output of the sample code illustrates, the pickled object is not a standard Python object.

NOTE: If the same object is dumped to a pickler object twice, only the first object is saved, even if the object has been modified.

```python
import cPickle

flights = {"1144":"Dallas", "1045":"Los Angeles", \
           "1520":"New York"}
times = ["230pm", "320pm", "420pm"]

#Create the pickle file
f = open("pickled.dat", "w")

#Create the pickler object
p = cPickle.Pickler(f)

#Pickle data to the file
p.dump(flights)
p.dump(times)
f.close()

#Display the file contents
f = open("pickled.dat", "r")
data = f.read()
print data
f.close()
```

pickle_data.py

```
(dp1
S'1520'
p2
S'New York'
p3
sS'1045'
p4
S'Los Angeles'
p5
sS'1144'
p6
S'Dallas'
p7
s.(lp8
S'230pm'
p9
aS'320pm'
p10
aS'420pm'
p11
a.
```

Output from pickle_data.py code

Unpickling Objects from a File

```
import cPickle
f = open("pickled.dat", "r")
p = cPickle.Unpickler(f)
data = p.load()
```

Pickling data to files is one of the simplest ways to get around the limitation that DBM files have of only allowing simple text string storage. The pickle and cPickle modules included with Python provide a simple-to-use interface to pickle entire objects to a file for persistent storage.

NOTE: The cPickler object is much faster than the pickler object; however, it will not allow you to subclass the pickler and unpickler objects for advanced handling of data.

The idea of unpickling is to read pickled objects from an existing pickle file and convert those pickled objects back to standard Python objects.

The first step in unpickling Python objects is to open the pickle file with the read permission. Once the file has been opened, use the UnPickler(*file*) method to create an unpickler object. The UnPickler method accepts a standard file object as its only parameter and returns the unpickler object that is used to read pickled objects from the file.

Once the unpickler object has been created, you can use the load() method to read a pickled object from the file. The object will be restructured and returned as a standard Python object.

```
import cPickle

#Open the pickle file
f = open("pickled.dat", "r")

#Create the unpickler object
p = cPickle.Unpickler(f)

#Unpickle an object from the file
data = p.load()
print "Flight Dictionary:"
print data

#Unpickle an object from the file
data = p.load()
```

```
print "\nTime List:"
print data

f.close()
```

unpickle_data.py

```
Flight Dictionary:
{'1520': 'New York', '1144': 'Dallas',
 '1045': 'Los Angeles'}

Time List:
['230pm', '320pm', '420pm']
```

Output from unpickle_data.py code

Storing Objects in a Shelve File

```
import shelve
db = shelve.open("shelved.dat", "n")
db['flights'] = flights
db['times'] = times
print db.keys()
```

Although pickling is great to store complex Python objects that DBMs cannot, it does not provide the direct entry access that is available with DBMs. Python provides the shelve module to bridge the gap and provide direct access to stored entries, as well as the ability to store complex Python objects. The shelve module accomplishes this by pickling the objects behind the scenes as they are added to the shelve file.

The shelve module provides its own open(*filename* [, *flags* [, *protocol* [, *writeback*]]]) method to create and open shelve files. The optional *flags* parameter accepts an r, w, c, or n character to determine whether the shelve will be read, write, created if it doesn't already exist, or truncated to zero length if it does exist. The optional *protocol* parameter accepts 0, 1, or 2 to determine whether the objects will be pickled as text based, binary, or a newer, faster method, respectively. The *writeback* parameter, which defaults to false, is a Boolean that, when set to true, causes changes to be cached until the database is closed.

The open method of the shelve module returns a shelve object that behaves much the same as a dictionary. Entries can be added to the shelve by assigning a value to a key using d[*key*] = *value*. The *key* must be a standard string; however, the *value* can be almost any Python object.

The output from the sample code shows what the contents of the shelve file looks like. You can see the objects in pickled form because the file was created using the default text-based protocol for pickling.

```
import shelve

flights = {"1144":"Dallas", "1045":"Los Angeles", \
           "1520":"New York"}
times = ["230pm", "320pm", "420pm"]

#Create shelve
db = shelve.open("shelved.dat", "n")

#Store objects in shelve
db['flights'] = flights
db['times'] = times

#Display added keys
```

```
print db.keys()

db.close()

#Display the file contents
f = open("shelved.dat", "r")
data = f.read()
print data
f.close()
```

shelve_store.py

```
['times', 'flights']

|(lp1
S'230pm'
p2
aS'320pm'
p3
aS'420pm'
p4
a.|times|(dp1
S'1520'
p2
S'New York'
p3
sS'1045'
p4
S'Los Angeles'
p5
sS'1144'
p6
S'Dallas'
p7
s.|flights
```

Output from shelve_store.py code

Retrieving Objects from a Shelve File

```
import shelve
db = shelve.open("shelved.dat", "r")
for k in db.keys():
    obj = db[k]
flightDB = db['flights']
flights = flightDB.keys()
cities = flightDB.values()
times = db['times']
```

The shelve module provides its own open(*filename* [, *flags* [, *protocol* [, *writeback*]]]) method to create and open shelve files. The optional *flags* parameter accepts an r, w, c, or n character to determine whether the shelve will be read, write, created if it doesn't already exist, or truncated to zero length if it does exist. The optional *protocol* parameter accepts 0, 1, or 2 to determine whether the objects will be pickled as text based, binary, or a newer, faster method, respectively. The *writeback* parameter which defaults to false, is a Boolean that, when set to true, causes changes to be cached until the database is closed.

NOTE: The optional *protocol* parameter accepts 0, 1, or 2 to determine whether the objects will be pickled as text based, binary, or a newer, faster method, respectively. When you open the shelve file to read objects, you must specify the correct protocol to properly unpickle the objects.

The open method of the shelve module opens a shelve file and returns a shelve object that behaves much the same as a dictionary. Once the shelve object has been created, you can use the shelve object similarly to a dictionary.

The keys() and values() functions retrieve a list of keys or values, respectively. You can also access a specific value by referencing using the corresponding key.

NOTE: When working with shelve files, the values that are returned can be almost any object type. You will need to keep this in mind when managing shelves that have multiple object types stored in them.

```python
import shelve

#Open shelve file
db = shelve.open("shelved.dat", "r")

#Get the keys from the shelve
for k in db.keys():
    obj = db[k]
    print "%s: %s" % (k, obj)

#Use keys to get values
flightDB = db['flights']
flights = flightDB.keys()
cities = flightDB.values()
times = db['times']

print "\nDepartures"
print
"==========================================="
x = 0
for flight in flights:
    print ("Flight %s leaves for %s at %s" % \
           (flight, cities[x],  times[x]))
    x+=1

db.close()
```

shelve_get.py

```
times: ['230pm', '320pm', '420pm']
flights: {'1520': 'New York', '1144': 'Dallas',
 '1045': 'Los Angeles'}

Departures
================================================
Flight 1520 leaves for New York at 230pm
Flight 1144 leaves for Dallas at 320pm
Flight 1045 leaves for Los Angeles at 420pm
```

Output from shelve_get.py code

Changing Objects in a Shelve File

```
import shelve
db = shelve.open("shelved.dat", "w", writeback=1)
flights = db['flights']
del flights['1144']
flights['1145'] = "Dallas"
db['times'] = newtimes
db.sync()
```

Once the shelve file has been opened, you can use the shelve object similarly to a dictionary. If you want to replace an existing object in the shelve with a new one, assign the new value to the corresponding key using d[key] = value. To remove an object from the database, use del d[key] to reference the object by its specific key.

Changing the value of specific parts of an object is where the power of using shelves rather than DBMs becomes very apparent. First, retrieve the object from the shelve by referencing its key using obj = d[key]. Once the object has been retrieved, values of the

object can be modified using standard Python. The
changes to the object are written back to the shelve
file automatically.

NOTE: In the example, we open the shelve with writeback set to true, so we use the `sync()` method of the
shelve module to force the changes to be flushed to
disk.

```python
import shelve

newtimes = ["110pm", "220pm", "300pm", "445pm"]

#Open shelve file
db = shelve.open("shelved.dat", "w", writeback=1)

#Get the keys
for k in db.keys():
    obj = db[k]
    print "%s: %s" % (k, obj)
print "\n\n"

#Use keys to get values
flights = db['flights']
times = db['times']

#Update contents of old object
del flights['1144']
flights['1145'] = "Dallas"
flights['1709'] = "Orlando"

#Replace old object with a new object
db['times'] = newtimes

#Add a new object
```

```
db['oldtimes'] = times

#Flush data to disk
db.sync()

for k in db.keys():
    obj = db[k]
    print "%s: %s" % (k, obj)

db.close()
```

shelve_edit.py

```
times: ['230pm', '320pm', '420pm']
flights: {'1520': 'New York', '1144': 'Dallas',
 '1045': 'Los Angeles'}

times: ['110pm', '220pm', '300pm', '445pm']
flights: {'1709': 'Orlando', '1520': 'New York',
 '1045': 'Los Angeles', '1145': 'Dallas'}
oldtimes: ['230pm', '320pm', '420pm']
```

Output from shelve_edit.py code

Connecting to a MySQL Database Server

```
import MySQLdb
myDB = MySQLdb.connect(host="127.0.0.1", \
                 port=3306)
cHandler = myDB.cursor()
```

The MySQLdb module provides the standard Python DB-API 2.0 specification connect([host= [, port= [, user= [, passwd= [, db= [, ...]]]]]]) function to connect to MySQL database servers. All the parameters to the connect function are optional. The most common parameters used are the host, port, user, passwd, and db.

Once you have successfully connected to the MySQL server, you need to get a cursor handle to send SQL requests to the server. The cursor() function returns a cursor object that can be used to execute SQL commands on the server and obtain the results.

To execute a SQL command on the server, use the execute(*operation* [, *parameters*]) function of the cursor object, where *operation* is basically any properly formatted SQL command string.

To retrieve the results from executing the command, use the fetchall() function of the cursor object. The fetchall function returns the results of the SQL request in a series of one or more lists depending on the data being returned.

Once you have the cursor object and are able to execute SQL commands, you can use the SHOW DATABASES SQL command to get a list of databases available on the server. To switch to a specific database, use the USE *<database>* SQL command.

NOTE: To find out which database is currently active, use the SELECT DATABASE() command to return the current database name.

```
import MySQLdb

#Connect to MySQL Server
myDB = MySQLdb.connect(host="127.0.0.1", \
```

```
                         port=3306)
cHandler = myDB.cursor()

#Display available databases
cHandler.execute("SHOW DATABASES")
results = cHandler.fetchall()
print"Databases\n===================="
for item in results:
    print item[0]

#Display current database
cHandler.execute("SELECT DATABASE()")
results = cHandler.fetchall()
print "\nCurrent Database\n======================="
for item in results:
    print item[0]

#Select database
cHandler.execute("USE schedule")

#Display current database
cHandler.execute("SELECT DATABASE()")
results = cHandler.fetchall()
print "\nCurrent Database\n======================="
for item in results:
    print item[0]

myDB.close()
```

MySQL_conn.py

```
Databases
====================
information_schema
airport
mysql
schedule
```

```
test
testy

Current Database
=======================
None

Current Database
=======================
schedule
```

Output from MySQL_conn.py code

Creating a MySQL Database

```
import MySQLdb
myDB = MySQLdb.connect(host="127.0.0.1", port=3306)
cHandler = myDB.cursor()
cHandler.execute("CREATE DATABASE schedule")
cHandler.execute("CREATE TABLE Arrivals (city TEXT,\
                        flight TEXT, time TEXT)")
```

Once you have connected to a MySQL database and got a SQL command cursor object, creating databases and tables is just a matter of sending the appropriately formatted SQL commands to the server.

To create a new database, use the execute(*operation* [, *parameters*]) function of the cursor object to initiate the CREATE DATABASE <*database*> SQL command. To create a new table, use the execute() function of the cursor object to initiate the CREATE Table <*tablename*> (<*column name*> <*column type*>, ...) SQL command.

To verify that the table has been created, use the SHOW TABLES SQL command to return a list of table entries available in the database.

NOTE: The table entries that are returned are in the form of a list. The first entry in the list is the table name.

To verify the structure of a specific table, use the DESCRIBE *<tablename>* SQL command to return a list of field entries included in the table.

NOTE: The field entries that are returned are in the form of a list. The first entry in the list is the field name and the second is the field type.

CAUTION: You must have appropriate permissions on the MySQL server to be able to create a database.

```
import MySQLdb

#Connect to MySQL Server
myDB = MySQLdb.connect(host="127.0.0.1", port=3306)

#Get the cursor object
cHandler = myDB.cursor()

#Create database
cHandler.execute("CREATE DATABASE schedule")

#Select database
cHandler.execute("USE schedule")

#Create table
cHandler.execute("CREATE TABLE Arrivals (city TEXT,\
                flight TEXT, time TEXT)")

#Show created table
```

```
cHandler.execute("SHOW TABLES")
results = cHandler.fetchall()
print results

#Describe the table
cHandler.execute("DESCRIBE Arrivals")
results = cHandler.fetchall()
print results

myDB.close()
```

MySQL_create.py

```
(('arrivals',),)

(('city', 'text', 'YES', '', None, ''),
('flight', 'text', 'YES', '', None, ''),
('time', 'text', 'YES', '', None, ''))
```

Output from MySQL_create.py code

Adding Entries to a MySQL Database

```
import MySQLdb
myDB = MySQLdb.connect(host="127.0.0.1", port=3306,
db="schedule")
cHandler = myDB.cursor()
    sqlCommand = "INSERT INTO Arrivals \
    VALUES('%s', '%s', '%s')" % \
    (city, flights[x], times[x])
    cHandler.execute(sqlCommand)
myDB.commit()
```

Once you have connected to a MySQL database and got a SQL command cursor object, adding entries to the database is just a matter of sending the appropriately formatted SQL commands to the server.

First, connect to the server using the MySQLdb modules connect function, and then use the MySQL database object to get a cursor object. In the sample code, entries are added one at a time by executing the INSERT INTO <tablename> VALUES (<data value>) SQL command using the execute function of the cursor object.

NOTE: Remember to use the commit() function of the cursor object to flush pending requests to the SQL database so that the changes will be written to disk.

```
import MySQLdb

cities = ["Dallas", "Los Angeles", "New York"]
flights = ["1144", "1045", "1520"]
times = ["230pm", "320pm", "420pm"]

#Connect to database
myDB = MySQLdb.connect(host="127.0.0.1", port=3306,
db="schedule")

#Get cursor object
cHandler = myDB.cursor()

#Add entries to database
x = 0
for city in cities:
    sqlCommand = "INSERT INTO Arrivals \
    VALUES('%s', '%s', '%s')" % \
    (city, flights[x], times[x])
    cHandler.execute(sqlCommand)
    x += 1
```

```
#View added entries
sqlCommand = "SELECT cities, flights, times FROM
Arrivals"
cHandler.execute(sqlCommand)
results = cHandler.fetchall()
print results

#Commit changes to database
myDB.commit()

myDB.close()
```

MySQL_add.py

```
(('Dallas', '1144', '230pm'),
('Los Angeles', '1045', '320pm'),
('New York', '1520', '420pm'))
```

Output from MySQL_add.py code

Retrieving Entries from a MySQL Database

```
import MySQLdb
myDB = MySQLdb.connect(host="127.0.0.1", port=3306,
db="schedule")
cHandler = myDB.cursor()
sqlCommand = "SELECT * FROM Arrivals"
cHandler.execute(sqlCommand)
results = cHandler.fetchall()
for row in results:
    cityList.append(row[0])
```

Once you have connected to a MySQL database and got a SQL command cursor object, retrieving entries from the database is just a matter of sending the appropriately formatted SQL commands to the server.

First, connect to the server using the MySQLdb modules `connect` function, and then use the MySQL database object to get a cursor object. In the sample code, all entries are retrieved together by executing the `SELECT * FROM <tablename>` SQL command using the `execute` function of the cursor object.

NOTE: The SELECT SQL command returns entries as a list of lists. Because we know that the field structure of the table is "city, flight, time," each field can be accessed directly using index 0, 1, and 2, respectively.

```
import MySQLdb

#Connect to database
myDB = MySQLdb.connect(host="127.0.0.1", \
                       port=3306, db="schedule")

#Get cursor object
cHandler = myDB.cursor()

#Send select request for specific entries
sqlCommand = "SELECT * FROM Arrivals \
 WHERE city = 'Dallas'"
cHandler.execute(sqlCommand)

#View results
results = cHandler.fetchall()
print results

#Send select request for all entries
sqlCommand = "SELECT * FROM Arrivals"
cHandler.execute(sqlCommand)

#View results
```

```
results = cHandler.fetchall()
print results

#Process rows into lists
cityList = []
flightList = []
timeList = []
for row in results:
    cityList.append(row[0])
    flightList.append(row[1])
    timeList.append(row[2])

print "\nArrivals"
print
"============================================="
x = 0
for flight in flightList:
    print ("Flight %s arrives from %s at %s" % \
            (flight, cityList[x],  timeList[x]))
    x+=1

myDB.close()
```

MySQL_get.py

```
(('Dallas', '1144', '230pm'),)

(('Dallas', '1144', '230pm'),
('Los Angeles', '1045', '320pm'),
('New York', '1520', '420pm'))

Arrivals
=============================================
Flight 1144 arrives from Dallas at 230pm
Flight 1045 arrives from Los Angeles at 320pm
Flight 1520 arrives from New York at 420pm
```

Output from MySQL_get.py code

7

Implementing Internet Communication

Python includes several built-in modules as well as add-on modules to implement different types of Internet communication. These modules simplify many of the tasks necessary to facilitate socket communication, email, file transfers, data streaming, HTTP requests, and more.

Because the communication possibilities with Python are so vast, this chapter focuses on phrases that implement simple socket servers, socket clients, and FTP clients, as well as POP3 and SMTP mail clients that can be easily incorporated into Python scripts.

Opening a Server-Side Socket for Receiving Data

```
sSock = socket(AF_INET, SOCK_STREAM)
sSock.bind((serverHost, serverPort))
sSock.listen(3)
conn, addr = sSock.accept()
data = conn.recv(1024)
```

The socket module included with Python provides a generic interface to a variety of low-level socket programming. This phrase discusses how to implement a low-level socket server using the socket module.

The first step in implementing a server-side socket interface is to create the server socket by calling -socket(*family*, *type* [, *proto*]), which creates and returns a new socket. *family* refers to the address family listed in Table 7.1, *type* refers to the socket types listed in Table 7.2, and *proto* refers to the protocol number, which is typically omitted except when working with raw sockets.

Table 7.1   Protocol Families for Python Sockets

Family	Description
AF_INET	Ipv4 protocols (TCP, UDP)
AF_INET6	Ipv6 protocols (TCP, UDP)
AF_UNIX	UNIX domain protocols

Table 7.2   Socket Types for Python Sockets

Type	Description
SOCK_STREAM	Opens an existing file for reading.
SOCK_DGRAM	Opens a file for writing. If the file already exists, the contents are deleted. If the file does not already exist, a new one is created.
SOCK_RAW	Opens an existing file for updating, keeping the existing contents intact.

Table 7.2   **Continued**

Type	Description
SOCK_RDM	Opens a file for both reading and writing. The existing contents are kept intact.
SOCK_SEQPACKET	Opens a file for both writing and reading. The existing contents are deleted.

Once the socket has been created, it must be bound to an address and port using the bind(*address*) method, where *address* refers to a tuple in the form of (*hostname*, *port*). If the hostname is an empty string, the server will allow connections on any available Internet interface on the system.

NOTE: You can specify <*broadcast*> as the hostname to use the socket to send broadcast messages.

After the socket has been bound to an interface, it can be activated by invoking the listen(*backlog*) method, where *backlog* is an integer that indicates how many pending connections the system should queue before rejecting new ones.

Once the socket is active, implement a while loop to wait for client connections using the accept() method. Once a client connection has been accepted, data can be read from the connection using the recv(*buffsize* [, *flags*]) method. The send(*string* [, *flags*]) method is used to write a response back to the client.

```
from socket import *

serverHost = '' # listen on all interfaces
serverPort = 50007

#Open socket to listen on
sSock = socket(AF_INET, SOCK_STREAM)
sSock.bind((serverHost, serverPort))
sSock.listen(3)

#Handle connections
while 1:

#Accept a connection
    conn, addr = sSock.accept()
    print 'Client Connection: ', addr
    while 1:

#Receive data
        data = conn.recv(1024)
        if not data: break
        print 'Server Received: ', data
        newData = data.replace('Client',
'Processed')

#Send response
        conn.send(newData)

#Close Connection
    conn.close()
```

server_socket.py

```
Client Connection:  ('137.65.77.24', 1678)
Server Received:  Client Message1
Server Received:  Client Message2
```

Output from server_socket.py code

Opening a Client-Side Socket for Sending Data

```
sSock = socket(AF_INET, SOCK_STREAM)
sSock.connect((serverHost, serverPort))
sSock.send(item)
data = sSock.recv(1024)
```

The socket module is also used to create a client-side socket that talks to the server-side socket discussed in the previous phrase.

The first step in implementing a client-side socket interface is to create the client socket by calling socket(*family*, *type* [, *proto*]), which creates and returns a new socket. *family* refers to the address family listed previously in Table 7.1, *type* refers to the socket types listed previously in Table 7.2, and *proto* refers to the protocol number, which is typically omitted except when working with raw sockets.

Once the client-side socket has been created, it can connect to the server socket using the connect(*address*) method, where *address* refers to a tuple in the form of (*hostname*, *port*).

NOTE: To connect to a server-socket on the local computer, use localhost as the hostname in the server address tuple.

After the client-side socket has connected to the server-side socket, data can be sent to the server using the send(*string* [,*flags*]) method. The response from the server is received from the connection using the recv(*buffsize* [,*flags*]) method.

```
import sys
from socket import *

serverHost = 'localhost'
serverPort = 50008

message = ['Client Message1', 'Client Message2']

if len(sys.argv) > 1:
    serverHost = sys.argv[1]

#Create a socket
sSock = socket(AF_INET, SOCK_STREAM)

#Connect to server
sSock.connect((serverHost, serverPort))

#Send messages
for item in message:
    sSock.send(item)
    data = sSock.recv(1024)
    print 'Client received: ', 'data'

sSock.close()
```

client_socket.py

```
Client received:    'Processed Message1'
Client received:    'Processed Message2'
```

Output from client_socket.py code

Receiving Streaming Data Using the ServerSocket Module

```
serv= SocketServer.TCPServer(("",50008),myTCPServer)
serv.serve_forever()
. . .
line = self.rfile.readline()
self.wfile.write("%s: %d bytes successfully \
received." % (sck, len(line)))
```

In addition to the socket module, Python includes the SocketServer module to provide you with TCP, UDP, and UNIX classes that implement servers. These classes have methods that provide you with a much higher level of socket control.

To implement a SocketServer to handle streaming requests, first define the class to inherit from the SocketServer.StreamRequestHandler class.

To handle the streaming requests, override the handle method to read and process the streaming data. The rfile.readline() function reads the streaming data until a newline character is encountered, and then returns the data as a string.

To send data back to the client from the streaming server, use the wfile.write(*string*) command to write the string back to the client.

Once you have defined the server class and overridden the handle method, create the server object by invoking SocketServer.TCPServer(*address, handler*), where *address* refers to a tuple in the form of (*hostname, port*) and *handler* refers to your defined server class.

After the server object has been created, you can start handling connections by invoking the server object's handle_request() or serve_forever() method.

> **NOTE:** In addition to the TCPServer method, you can
> also use the UDPServer, UnixStreamServer, and
> UnixDatagramServer methods to create other types of
> servers.

```python
import socket
import string

class
myTCPServer(SocketServer.StreamRequestHandler):
    def handle (self):
        while 1:
            peer = self.connection.getpeername()[0]
            line = self.rfile.readline()
            print "%s wrote: %s" % (peer, line)
            sck = self.connection.getsockname()[0]
            self.wfile.write("%s: %d bytes \
                successfuly received." % \
                (sck, len(line)))

#Create SocketServer object
serv =
SocketServer.TCPServer(("",50008),myTCPServer)

#Activate the server to handle clients
serv.serve_forever()
```

stream_server.py

```
137.65.76.8 wrote: Hello
137.65.76.8 wrote: Here is today's weather.
137.65.76.8 wrote: Sunny
137.65.76.8 wrote: High: 75
137.65.76.8 wrote: Low: 58
137.65.76.8 wrote: bye
```

Output from stream_server.py code

Sending Streaming Data

```
sSock = socket(AF_INET, SOCK_STREAM)
sSock.connect((serverHost, serverPort))
line = raw_input("Send to %s: " % (serverHost))
sSock.send(line+'\n')
data = sSock.recv(1024)
```

To send streaming data to the streaming server described in the previous task, first create the client socket by calling socket(*family*, *type* [, *proto*]), which creates and returns a new socket.

Once the streaming client-side socket has been created, it can connect to the streaming server using the connect(*address*) method, where *address* refers to a tuple in the form of (*hostname*, *port*).

After the streaming client-side socket has connected to the server-side socket, data can be streamed to the server by formatting a stream of data that ends with the newline character and sending it to the server using the send(*string* [,*flags*]) method.

A response from the server is received from the socket using the recv(*buffsize* [,*flags*]) method.

```
import sys
from socket import *

serverHost = 'localhost'
serverPort = 50008

if len(sys.argv) > 1:
    serverHost = sys.argv[1]

#Create socket
sSock = socket(AF_INET, SOCK_STREAM)

#Connect to server
```

```
sSock.connect((serverHost, serverPort))

#Stream data to server.
line = ""
while line != 'bye':
    line = raw_input("Send to %s: " % (serverHost))
    sSock.send(line+'\n')
    data = sSock.recv(1024)
    print 'data'

sSock.shutdown(0)
sSock.close()
```

stream_client.py

```
Send to 137.65.76.28: Hello
'137.65.77.28: 6 bytes received.'
Send to 137.65.76.28: Here is today's weather.
'137.65.77.28: 25 bytes received.'
Send to 137.65.76.28: Sunny
'137.65.77.28: 6 bytes received.'
Send to 137.65.76.28: High: 75
'137.65.77.28: 9 bytes received.'
Send to 137.65.76.28: Low: 58
'137.65.77.28: 8 bytes received.'
Send to 137.65.76.28: bye
'137.65.77.28: 4 bytes received.'
```

Output from stream_client.py code

Sending Email Using SMTP

```
mMessage = ('From: %s\nTo: %s\nDate: %s\nSubject:\
            %s\n%s\n' % \
            (From, To, Date, Subject, Text))
s = smtplib.SMTP('mail.sfcn.org')
rCode = s.sendmail(From, To, mMessage)
s.quit()
```

The smtplib module included with Python provides simple access to SMTP servers that allow you to connect and quickly send mail messages from your Python scripts.

Mail messages must be formatted properly for the To, From, Date, Subject, and text fields to be processed properly by the SMTP mail server. The code in send_smtp.py shows the proper formatting for the mail message, including the item headers and newline characters.

Once the mail message is properly formatted, connect to the SMTP server using the smtplib.SMTP(*host* [,*port*]) method. If it is necessary to log in to the SMTP server, use the login(*user*, *password*) method to complete an authentication.

Once connected to the SMTP server, the formatted message can be sent using sendmail(*from*, *to*, *message*), where *from* is the sending email address string, *to* specifies a list of destination email address strings, and *message* is the formatted message string.

After you are finished sending messages, use the quit() method to close the connection to the SMTP server.

```python
import smtplib
import time

From = "bwdayley@sfcn.org"
To = ["bwdayley@novell.com"]
Date = time.ctime(time.time())
Subject = "New message from Brad Dayley."
Text = "Message Text"
#Format mail message
mMessage = ('From: %s\nTo: %s\nDate: \
            %s\nSubject: %s\n%s\n' %
```

```
              (From, To, Date, Subject, Text))

print 'Connecting to Server'
s = smtplib.SMTP('mail.sfcn.org')

#Send mail
rCode = s.sendmail(From, To, mMessage)
s.quit()

if rCode:
    print 'Error Sending Message'
else:
    print 'Message Sent Successfully'
```

send_smtp.py

```
Connecting to Server
Message Sent Successfully
```

Output from send_smtp.py code

Also see Figure 7.1.

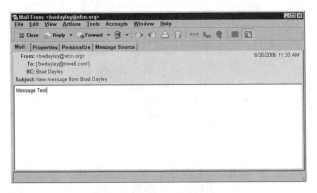

Figure 7.1   Email message sent by send_smtp.py code.

Retrieving Email from a POP3 Server

```
mServer = poplib.POP3('mail.sfcn.org')
mServer.user(getpass.getuser())
mServer.pass_(getpass.getpass())
numMessages = len(mServer.list()[1])
for msg in mServer.retr(mList+1)[1]:
```

The poplib module included with Python provides simple access to POP3 mail servers that allow you to connect and quickly retrieve messages using your Python scripts.

Connect to the POP3 mail server using the `poplib.POP3(host [,port [,keyfile [,certfile]]])` method, where *host* is the address of the POP3 mail server. The optional *port* argument defaults to 995. The other optional arguments, *keyfile* and *certfile*, refer to the PEM-formatted private key and certificate authentication files, respectively.

To log in to the POP3 server, the code in pop3_mail.py calls the `user(username)` and `pass_(password)` methods of the POP3 server object to complete the authentication.

NOTE: The example uses `getuser()` and `getpass()` from the getpass module to retrieve the username and password. The username and password can also be passed in as clear text strings.

After it's authenticated to the POP3 server, the poplib module provides several methods to manage the mail messages. The example uses the `list()` method to retrieve a list of messages in the tuple format (*response*, *msglist*, *size*), where *response* is the server's response code, *msglist* is a list of messages in string format, and *size* is the size of the response in bytes.

To retrieve only a single message, use retr(*msgid*). The retr method returns the message numbered msgid in the form of a tuple (*response*, *lines*, *size*), where *response* is the server response, *lines* is a list of strings that compose the mail message, and *size* is the total size in bytes of the message.

NOTE: The *lines* list returned by the retr method includes all lines of the messages, including the header. To retrieve specific information, such as the recipient list, the *lines* list must be parsed.

When you are finished managing the mail messages, use the quit() method to close the connection to the POP3 server.

```
import poplib
import getpass

mServer = poplib.POP3('mail.sfcn.org')

#Login to mail server
mServer.user(getpass.getuser())
mServer.pass_(getpass.getpass())

#Get the number of mail messages
numMessages = len(mServer.list()[1])

print "You have %d messages." % (numMessages)
print "Message List:"

#List the subject line of each message
for mList in range(numMessages) :
    for msg in mServer.retr(mList+1)[1]:
        if msg.startswith('Subject'):
            print '\t' + msg
```

```
          break

mServer.quit()
```

pop3_mail.py

```
password:
You have 10 messages.
Message List:
    Subject: Static IP Info
    Subject: IP Address Change
    Subject: Verizon Wireless Online Statement
    Subject: New Static IP Address
    Subject: Your server account has been created
    Subject: Looking For New Home Projects?
    Subject: PDF Online - cl_scr_sheet.xls
    Subject: Professional 11 Upgrade Offer
    Subject: #1 Ball Played at the U.S. Open
    Subject: Chapter 3 submission
```

Output from pop3_mail.py code

Using Python to Fetch Files from an FTP Server

```
ftp = ftplib.FTP('ftp.novell.com', 'anonymous', \
                 'bwdayley@novell.com')
gFile = open("readme.txt", "wb")
ftp.retrbinary('RETR Readme', gFile.write)
gFile.close()
ftp.quit()
```

A common and extremely useful function of Python scripts is to retrieve files to be processed using the FTP protocol. The ftplib module included in Python allows you to use Python scripts to quickly attach to an FTP server, locate files, and then download them to be processed locally.

To open a connection to the FTP server, create an FTP server object using the `ftplib.FTP([`*host* `[, ` *user* `[, ` *passwd*`]]])` method.

Once the connection to the server is opened, the methods in the ftplib module provide most of the FTP functionality to navigate the directory structure, manage files and directories, and, of course, download files.

The example shows connecting to an FTP server, listing the files and directories in the FTP server root directory using the `dir()` method, and then changing the directory using the `cwd(`*path*`)` method. In the example, the contents of the file Readme are downloaded from the FTP server and written to the local file readme.txt using the `retrbinary(`*command*`, ` *callback* `[, ` *blocksize* `[, ` *reset*`]])` method.

After you are finished downloading/managing the files on the FTP server, use the `quit()` method to close the connection.

```
import ftplib

#Open ftp connection
ftp = ftplib.FTP('ftp.novell.com', 'anonymous',
'bwdayley@novell.com')

#List the files in the current directory
print "File List:"
files = ftp.dir()
print files


#Get the readme file
```

```
ftp.cwd("/pub")
gFile = open("readme.txt", "wb")
ftp.retrbinary('RETR Readme', gFile.write)
gFile.close()
ftp.quit()

#Print the readme file contents
print "\nReadme File Output:"
gFile = open("readme.txt", "r")
buff = gFile.read()
print buff
gFile.close()
```

ftp_client.py

```
File List:
-rw-r-r- 1 root root  720 Dec 15  2005 README.html
-rw-r-r- 1 root root 1406 Dec 15  2005 Readme
drwxrwxrwx 2 root root 53248 Jun 26 18:10 incoming
drwxrwxrwx 2 root root 16384 Jun 26 17:53 outgoing
drwxr-xr-x 3 root root  4096 May 12 16:12 partners
drwxr-xr-x 2 root root  4096 Apr  4 18:24 priv
drwxr-xr-x 4 root root  4096 May 25 22:20 pub
None

Readme File Output:
***************************************************

 Before you download any software product you must
 read and agree to the following:
. . .
```

Output from ftp_client.py code

8

Processing HTML

Several modules included with Python provide virtually all the necessary tools necessary to parse and process HTML documents without needing to use a web server or web browser. Parsing HTML files is becoming much more commonplace in such applications as search engines, document indexing, document conversion, data retrieval, site backup or migration, as well as several others.

Because there is no way to cover the extent of options Python provides in HTML processing, the first two phrases in this chapter focus on specific Python modules to simplify opening HTML documents locally and on the Web. The rest of the phrases discuss how to use the Python modules to quickly parse the data in the HTML files to process specific items, such as links, images, and cookies. The final phrase in this chapter uses the example of fixing HTML files that do not have properly formatted tag data to demonstrate how to easily process the entire contents of the HTML file.

Parsing URLs

```
import urlparse
parsedTuple = urlparse.urlparse(
"http://www.google.com/search?
hl=en&q=urlparse&btnG=Google+Search")
unparsedURL = urlparse.urlunparse((URLscheme, \
        URLlocation, URLpath, '', '', ''))
newURL = urlparse.urljoin(unparsedURL,
"/module-urllib2/request-objects.html")
```

The urlparse module included with Python makes it
easy to break down URLs into specific components
and reassemble them. This is very useful for a number
of purposes when processing HTML documents.

The urlparse(*urlstring* [, *default_scheme* [,
allow_fragments]]) function takes the URL provided
in *urlstring* and returns the tuple *(scheme, netloc,
path, parameters, query, fragment)*. The tuple can
then be used to determine things such as location
scheme (HTTP, FTP, and so on), server address, file
path, and so on.

The urlunparse(*tuple*) function accepts the tuple
(scheme, netloc, path, parameters, query, fragment)
and reassembles it into a properly formatted URL that
can be used by the other HTML parsing modules
included with Python.

The urljoin(*base, url* [, *allow_fragments*]) function
accepts a base URL as the first argument and then
joins whatever relative URL is specified in the second
argument. The urljoin function is extremely useful in
processing several files in the same location by joining
new filenames to the existing base URL location.

NOTE: If the relative path does not start using the root (/) character, the rightmost location in the base URL path will be replaced with the relative path. For example, a base URL of http://www.testpage.com/pub and a relative URL of test.html would join to form the URL http://www.testpage.com/test.html, not http://www.testpage.com/test.html. If you want to keep the end directory in the path, make sure to end the base URL string with a / character.

```
import urlparse

URLscheme = "http"
URLlocation = "www.python.org"
URLpath = "lib/module-urlparse.html"

modList = ("urllib", "urllib2", \
           "httplib", "cgilib")

#Parse address into tuple
print "Parsed Google search for urlparse"
parsedTuple = urlparse.urlparse(
"http://www.google.com/search?
hl=en&q=urlparse&btnG=Google+Search")
print parsedTuple

#Unparse list into URL
print "\nUnparsed python document page"
unparsedURL = urlparse.urlunparse( \
(URLscheme, URLlocation, URLpath, '', '', ''))
print "\t" + unparsedURL

#Join path to new file to create new URL
print "\nAdditional python document pages using
join"
for mod in modList:
```

```
    newURL = urlparse.urljoin(unparsedURL, \
                    "module-%s.html" % (mod))
    print "\t" + newURL

#Join path to subpath to create new URL
print "\nPython document pages using join of sub-
path"
newURL = urlparse.urljoin(unparsedURL,
        "module-urllib2/request-objects.html")
print "\t" + newURL
```

URL_parse.py

```
Parsed Google search for urlparse
('http', 'www.google.com', '/search', '',
'hl=en&q=urlparse&btnG=Google+Search', '')

Unparsed python document page
        http://www.python.org/lib/module-
urlparse.html

Additional python document pages using join
        http://www.python.org/lib/module-urllib.html
        http://www.python.org/lib/module-urllib2.html
        http://www.python.org/lib/module-httplib.html
        http://www.python.org/lib/module-cgilib.html

Python document pages using join of sub-path
        http://www.python.org/lib/module-urllib2/
request-objects.html
```

Output from URL_parse.py code

Opening HTML Documents

```
import urllib
u = urllib.urlopen(webURL)
u = urllib.urlopen(localURL)
buffer = u.read()
print u.info()
print "Read %d bytes from %s.\n" % \
(len(buffer), u.geturl())
```

The urllib and urllib2 modules included with Python provide the functionality to open and fetch data from URLs, including HTML documents.

To use the urllib module to open an HTML document, specify the URL location of the document, including the filename in the urlopen(url [,data]) function. The urlopen function will open a local file and return a file-like object that can be used to read data from the HTML document.

Once you have opened the HTML document, you can read the file using the read([nbytes]), readline(), and readlines() functions similar to normal files. To read the entire contents of the HTML document, use the read() function to return the file contents as a string.

After you open a location, you can retrieve the location of the file using the geturl() function. The geturl function returns the URL in string format, taking into account any redirection that might have taken place when accessing the HTML file.

NOTE: Another helpful function included in the file-like object returned from urlopen is the info() function. The info() function returns the available metadata about the URL location, including content length, content type, and so on.

```python
import urllib

webURL = "http://www.python.org"
localURL = "/books/python/CH8/code/test.html"

#Open web-based URL
u = urllib.urlopen(webURL)
buffer = u.read()
print u.info()
print "Read %d bytes from %s.\n" % \
(len(buffer), u.geturl())

#Open local-based URL
u = urllib.urlopen(localURL)
buffer = u.read()
print u.info()
print "Read %d bytes from %s." % \
(len(buffer), u.geturl())
```

html_open.py

```
Date: Tue, 18 Jul 2006 18:28:19 GMT
Server: Apache/2.0.54 (Debian GNU/Linux)
DAV/2 SVN/1.1.4 mod_python/3.1.3 Python/2.3.5
mod_ssl/2.0.54 OpenSSL/0.9.7e
Last-Modified: Mon, 17 Jul 2006 23:06:04 GMT
ETag: "601f6-351c-1310af00"
Accept-Ranges: bytes
Content-Length: 13596
Connection: close
Content-Type: text/html

Web-Based URL
Read 13596 bytes from http://www.python.org.
Content-Type: text/html
Content-Length: 433
```

```
Last-modified: Thu, 13 Jul 2006 22:07:53 GMT

Local-Based URL
Read 433 bytes from
file:///books/python/CH8/code/test.html.
```

Output from html_open.py code

Retrieving Links from HTML Documents

```python
import HTMLParser
import urllib
class parseLinks(HTMLParser.HTMLParser):
    def handle_starttag(self, tag, attrs):
        if tag == 'a':
            for name,value in attrs:
                if name == 'href':
                    print value
                    print self.get_starttag_text()

lParser = parseLinks()
lParser.feed(urllib.urlopen( \
    "http://www.python.org/index.html").read())
```

The Python language comes with a very useful
HTMLParser module that enables simple, efficient parsing of HTML documents based on the tags inside the
HTML document. The HTMLParser module is one of
the most important when processing HTML documents.

A common task when processing HTML documents is
to pull all the links out of the document. Using the
HTMLParser module, this task is fairly simple. The first
step is to define a new HTMLParser class that overrides the handle_starttag() method to print the href
attribute value of all a tags.

Once the new HTMLParser class has been defined, create an instance of the class to return an HTMLParser object. Then open the HTML document using urllib.urlopen(url) and read the contents of the HTML file.

To parse the HTML file contents and print the links contained inside, feed the data to the HTMLParser object using the feed(data) function. The feed function of the HTMLParser object will accept the data and parse it based on the defined HTMLParser object.

NOTE: If the data passed to the feed() function of the HTMLParser is not complete, the incomplete tag is kept and then parsed the next time the feed() function is called. This can be useful when working with large HTML files that need to be fed to the parser in chunks.

```python
import HTMLParser
import urllib
import sys

#Define HTML Parser
class parseLinks(HTMLParser.HTMLParser):
    def handle_starttag(self, tag, attrs):
        if tag == 'a':
            for name,value in attrs:
                if name == 'href':
                    print value
                    print self.get_starttag_text()

#Create instance of HTML parser
lParser = parseLinks()

#Open the HTML file
lParser.feed(urllib.urlopen( \
```

```
    "http://www.python.org/index.html").read())

lParser.close()
```

html_links.py

```
<a href="psf" class=""
title="Python Software Foundation">
links
<a href="links" class="" title="">
dev
<a href="dev" class=""
title="Python Core Language Development">
download/releases/2.4.3
<a href="download/releases/2.4.3">
http://docs.python.org
<a href="http://docs.python.org">
ftp/python/2.4.3/python-2.4.3.msi
<a href="ftp/python/2.4.3/python-2.4.3.msi">
ftp/python/2.4.3/Python-2.4.3.tar.bz2
<a href="ftp/python/2.4.3/Python-2.4.3.tar.bz2">
pypi
```

Output from html_links.py code

Retrieving Images from HTML Documents

```
import HTMLParser
import urllib

def getImage(addr):
    u = urllib.urlopen(addr)
    data = u.read()

class parseImages(HTMLParser.HTMLParser):
```

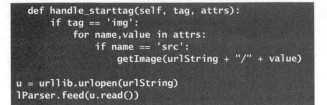

```
    def handle_starttag(self, tag, attrs):
        if tag == 'img':
            for name,value in attrs:
                if name == 'src':
                    getImage(urlString + "/" + value)

u = urllib.urlopen(urlString)
lParser.feed(u.read())
```

A common task when processing HTML documents is to pull all the images out of the document. Using the HTMLParser module, this task is fairly simple. The first step is to define a new HTMLParser class that overrides the handle_starttag() method to find the img tags and saves the file pointed to by the src attribute value.

Once the new HTMLParser class has been defined, create an instance of the class to return an HTMLParser object. Then open the HTML document using urllib.urlopen(url) and read the contents of the HTML file.

To parse the HTML file contents and save the images displayed inside, feed the data to the HTMLParser object using the feed(data) function. The feed function of the HTMLParser object will accept the data and parse it based on the defined HTMLParser object.

```
import HTMLParser
import urllib
import sys

urlString = "http://www.python.org"

#Save image file to disk
def getImage(addr):
    u = urllib.urlopen(addr)
```

```
    data = u.read()

    splitPath = addr.split('/')
    fName = splitPath.pop()
    print "Saving %s" % fName

    f = open(fName, 'wb')
    f.write(data)
    f.close()

#Define HTML parser
class parseImages(HTMLParser.HTMLParser):
    def handle_starttag(self, tag, attrs):
        if tag == 'img':
            for name,value in attrs:
                if name == 'src':
                    getImage(urlString + "/" +
value)

#Create instance of HTML parser
lParser = parseImages()

#Open the HTML file
u = urllib.urlopen(urlString)
print "Opening URL\n===================="
print u.info()

#Feed HTML file into parser
lParser.feed(u.read())

lParser.close()
```

html_images.py

```
Opening URL
====================
Date: Wed, 19 Jul 2006 18:47:27 GMT
```

```
Server: Apache/2.0.54 (Debian GNU/Linux)
DAV/2 SVN/1.1.4 mod_python/3.1.3 Python/2.3.5
mod_ssl/2.0.54 OpenSSL/0.9.7e
Last-Modified: Wed, 19 Jul 2006 16:08:34 GMT
ETag: "601f6-351c-79a6c480"
Accept-Ranges: bytes
Content-Length: 13596
Connection: close
Content-Type: text/html

Saving python-logo.gif
Saving trans.gif
Saving trans.gif
Saving nasa.jpg
```

Output from html_images.py code

Retrieving Text from HTML Documents

```
import HTMLParser
import urllib

class parseText(HTMLParser.HTMLParser):
    def handle_data(self, data):
        if data != '\n':
            urlText.append(data)

lParser = parseText()
lParser.feed(urllib.urlopen( \
http://docs.python.org/lib/module-HTMLParser.html \
).read())
```

A common task when processing HTML documents is to pull all the text out of the document. Using the HTMLParser module, this task is fairly simple. The first step is to define a new HTMLParser class that overrides the `handle_data()` method to parse and print the text data.

Once the new HTMLParser class has been defined, create an instance of the class to return an HTMLParser object. Then open the HTML document using `urllib.urlopen(url)` and read the contents of the HTML file.

To parse the HTML file contents and print the text contained inside, feed the HTML file contents to the HTMLParser object using the `feed(data)` function. The `feed` function of the HTMLParser object will accept the data and parse it based on the defined HTMLParser object.

NOTE: If the data passed to the `feed()` function of the HTMLParser is not complete, the incomplete tag is kept and then parsed the next time the `feed()` function is called. This can be useful when working with large HTML files that need to be fed to the parser in chunks.

```python
import HTMLParser
import urllib

urlText = []

#Define HTML Parser
class parseText(HTMLParser.HTMLParser):
    def handle_data(self, data):
        if data != '\n':
            urlText.append(data)


#Create instance of HTML parser
```

```
lParser = parseText()

#Feed HTML file into parser
lParser.feed(urllib.urlopen( \
http://docs.python.org/lib/module-HTMLParser.html \
).read())
lParser.close()
for item in urlText:
    print item
```

html_text.py

```
13.1 HTMLParser — Simple HTML and XHTML parser
Python Library Reference
Previous:
13. Structured Markup Processing
Up:
13. Structured Markup Processing
Next:
13.1.1 Example HTML Parser

13.1
HTMLParser
  —
        Simple HTML and XHTML parser
. . .
```

Output from html_text.py code

Retrieving Cookies in HTML Documents

```
import urllib2
import cookielib
from urllib2 import urlopen, Request

cJar = cookielib.LWPCookieJar()
```

```
opener=urllib2.build_opener( \
    urllib2.HTTPCookieProcessor(cJar))
urllib2.install_opener(opener)
r = Request(testURL)
h = urlopen(r)
for ind, cookie in enumerate(cJar):
    print "%d - %s" % (ind, cookie)
    cJar.save(cookieFile)
```

The Python language includes a cookielib module that provides classes for automatic handling of HTTP cookies in HTML documents. This can be absolutely necessary when dealing with HTML documents that require cookies to be set on the client.

To retrieve the cookies from an HTML document, first create an instance of a cookie jar using the LWPCookieJar() function of the cookielib module. The LWPCookieJar() function returns an object that can load from and save cookies to disk.

Next, create an opener, using the build_opener ([handler, . . .]) function of the urllib2 module, which will handle the cookies when the HTML file is opened. The build_opener function accepts zero or more handlers that will be chained together in the order in which they are specified and returns an opener object.

NOTE: If you want urlopen() to use the opener object to open HTML files, call the install_opener(opener) function and pass in the opener object. Otherwise, use the open(url) function of the opener object to open the HTML files.

Once the opener has been created and installed, create a Request object using the Request(url) function of the urllib2 module, and then open the HTML file using the urlopen(request) function.

Once the HTML page has been opened, any cookies in the page will now be stored in the LWPCookieJar object. You can then use the save(*filename*) function of the LWPCookieJar object.

```
import os
import urllib2
import cookielib
from urllib2 import urlopen, Request

cookieFile = "cookies.dat"
testURL = 'http://maps.google.com/'

#Create instance of cookie jar
cJar = cookielib.LWPCookieJar()

#Create HTTPCookieProcessor opener object
opener = urllib2.build_opener( \
    urllib2.HTTPCookieProcessor(cJar))

#Install the HTTPCookieProcessor opener
urllib2.install_opener(opener)

#Create a Request object
r = Request(testURL)

#Open the HTML file
h = urlopen(r)
print "Page Header\n======================="
print h.info()

print "Page Cookies\n======================="
for ind, cookie in enumerate(cJar):
    print "%d - %s" % (ind, cookie)

#Save the cookies
cJar.save(cookieFile)
```

html_cookie.py

```
Page Header
======================
Cache-Control: private
Set-Cookie: PREF=ID=fac1f1fcb33dae16:TM=1153336398:
LM=1153336398:S=CpIvoPKTNq6KhCx1; expires=Sun,
17-Jan-2038 19:14:07 GMT; path=/; domain=.google.com
Content-Type: text/html; charset=ISO-8859-1
Server: mfe
Content-Length: 28271
Date: Wed, 19 Jul 2006 19:13:18 GMT

Page Cookies
======================
0 - <Cookie PREF=ID=fac1f1fcb33dae16:TM=1153336398:
LM=1153336398:S=CpIvoPKTNq6KhCx1 for .google.com/>
```

Output from html_cookie.py code

Adding Quotes to Attribute Values in HTML Documents

```
import HTMLParser
import urllib

class parseAttrs(HTMLParser.HTMLParser):
    def handle_starttag(self, tag, attrs):
        . . .

attrParser = parseAttrs()
attrParser.init_parser()
attrParser.feed(urllib.urlopen("test2.html").read())
```

Earlier in this chapter, we discussed parsing HTML files based on specific handlers in the HTML parser. There are times when you need to use all the handlers to process an HTML document. Using the HTMLParser module to parse all entities in the

HTML file is not much more complex than handling links or images.

This phrase discusses how to use the HTMLParser module to parse an HTML file to fix the fact that the attribute values do not have quotes around them. The first step is to define a new HTMLParser class that overrides all the following handlers so that the quotes can be added to the attribute values:

```
handle_starttag(tag, attrs)
handle_charref(name)
handle_endtag(tag)
handle_entityref(ref)
handle_data(text)
handle_comment(text)
handle_pi(text)
handle_decl(text)
handle_startendtag(tag, attrs)
```

You will also need to define a function inside the parser class to initialize the variables used to store the parsed data and another function to return the parsed data.

Once the new HTMLParser class has been defined, create an instance of the class to return an HTMLParser object. Use the init function you created to initialize the parser; then open the HTML document using urllib.urlopen(url) and read the contents of the HTML file.

To parse the HTML file contents and add the quotes to the attribute values, feed the data to the HTMLParser object using the feed(data) function. The feed function of the HTMLParser object will accept the data and parse it based on the defined HTMLParser object.

```
import HTMLParser
import urllib
import sys

#Define the HTML parser
class parseAttrs(HTMLParser.HTMLParser):
    def init_parser (self):
        self.pieces = []

    def handle_starttag(self, tag, attrs):
        fixedAttrs = ""
        #for name,value in attrs:
        for name, value in attrs:
            fixedAttrs += "%s=\"%s\" " % (name,
value)
        self.pieces.append("<%s %s>" % (tag,
fixedAttrs))

    def handle_charref(self, name):
        self.pieces.append("&#%s;" % (name))

    def handle_endtag(self, tag):
        self.pieces.append("</%s>" % (tag))

    def handle_entityref(self, ref):
        self.pieces.append("&%s" % (ref))

    def handle_data(self, text):
        self.pieces.append(text)

    def handle_comment(self, text):
        self.pieces.append("<!-%s->" % (text))

    def handle_pi(self, text):
        self.pieces.append("<?%s>" % (text))
```

```python
    def handle_decl(self, text):
        self.pieces.append("<!%s>" % (text))

    def parsed (self):
        return "".join(self.pieces)

#Create instance of HTML parser
attrParser = parseAttrs()

#Initialize the parser data
attrParser.init_parser()

#Feed HTML file into parser
attrParser.feed(urllib.urlopen("test2.html").read())

#Display original file contents
print "Original File\n========================"
print open("test2.html").read()

#Display the parsed file
print "Parsed File\n========================"
print attrParser.parsed()

attrParser.close()
```

html_quotes.py

```
Original File
========================
<html lang="en" xml:lang="en">
<head>
<meta content="text/html; charset=utf-8"
 http-equiv="content-type" />
<title>Web Page</title>
</head>
<body>
<H1>Web Listings</H1>
<a href=http://www.python.org>Python Web Site</a>
```

```
<a href=test.html>local page</a>
<img SRC=test.jpg>
</body>
</html>

Parsed File
=========================
<html lang="en" xml:lang="en" >
<head >
<meta content="text/html; charset=utf-8"
 http-equiv="content-type" ></meta>
<title >Web Page</title>
</head>
<body >
<h1 >Web Listings</h1>
<a href="http://www.python.org" >Python Web Site</a>
<a href="test.html" >local page</a>
<img src="test.jpg" >
</body>
</html>
```

Output from html_quotes.py code

9

Processing XML

Python includes several modules that provide most of the tools necessary to parse and process XML documents. Parsing XML files is becoming much more critical as applications adopt the XML standard as the best way to transfer data between applications and systems.

Because there is no way to cover the extent of options Python provides in XML processing, I've chosen to present phrases that demonstrate some common tasks. To provide as broad of coverage as possible, these phrases will use the xml.dom, xml.sax, and xml.parsers.expat modules.

The phrases in this chapter cover concepts of basic XML processing such as loading, navigating, and checking for well-formed documents. They also cover more advanced XML processing such as searches, tag processing, and extracting text.

NOTE: Many XML processing tasks could be accomplished differently by using different modules. Don't get locked into a specific module for processing the XML data; another module may perform the same task better.

NOTE: All the phrases in this chapter process the same XML file. The output of that XML file is listed in the output section of the "Loading an XML Document" phrase.

Loading an XML Document

```
from xml.dom import minidom
DOMTree = minidom.parse('emails.xml')
print DOMTree.toxml()
```

The easiest way to quickly load an XML document is to create a minidom object using the xml.dom module. The minidom object provides a simple parser method that will quickly create a DOM tree from the XML file.

The sample phrase calls the parse(*file* [,*parser*]) function of the minidom object to parse the XML file designated by *file* into a DOM tree object. The optional *parser* argument allows you to specify a custom parser object to use when parsing the XML file.

NOTE: The DOM tree object can be converted back into XML by calling the toxml() function of the object, which returns a string containing the full contents of the XML file.

```
from xml.dom import minidom

#Open XML document using minidom parser
DOMTree = minidom.parse('emails.xml')

#Print XML contents
print DOMTree.toxml()
```

xml_open.py

```xml
<?xml version="1.0" ?><!DOCTYPE emails [
        <!ELEMENT email (to, from, subject,
 date, body)>
        <!ELEMENT to (addr+)>
        <!ELEMENT from (addr)>
        <!ELEMENT subject (#PCDATA)>
        <!ELEMENT date (#PCDATA)>
        <!ELEMENT body (#PCDATA)>
        <!ELEMENT addr (#PCDATA)>
        <!ATTLIST addr type (FROM | TO |
 CC | BC) "none">
    ]><emails>
    <email>
        <to>
            <addr
type="TO">bwdayley@novell.com</addr>
            <addr type="CC">bwdayley@sfcn.org</addr>
        </to>
        <from>
            <addr
type="FROM">ddayley@sfcn.org</addr>
        </from>
        <subject>
        Update List
        </subject>
        <body>
        Please add me to the list.
        </body>
    </email>
    <email>
        <to>
            <addr
type="TO">bwdayley@novell.com</addr>
            <addr type="BC">bwdayley@sfcn.org</addr>
        </to>
        <from>
            <addr
```

```
type="FROM">cdayley@sfcn.org</addr>
        </from>
        <subject>
        More Updated List
        </subject>
        <body>
        Please add me to the list also.
        </body>
    </email>
</emails>
```

Output from xml_open.py code

Checking for Well-Formed XML Documents

```
from xml.sax.handler import ContentHandler
import xml.sax
xmlparser = xml.sax.make_parser()
xmlparser.setContentHandler(ContentHandler())
xmlparser.parse(fName)
```

One of the most common tasks when processing XML documents is checking to see whether a document is well formed. The best way to determine whether a document is well formed is to use the xml.sax module to parse inside a try statement that will handle an exception if the document is not well formed.

First, create an xml.sax parser object using the make_parser() function. The make_parser function will return a parser object that can be used to parse the XML file.

After you have created the parser object, add a content handler to the object using its setContentHandler (*handler*) function. In this phrase, a generic content handler is passed to the object by calling the `xml.sax.handler.ContentHandler()` function.

Once the content handler has been added to the parser object, the XML files can be parsed inside a `try` block. If the parser encounters an error in the XML document, an exception will be thrown; otherwise, the document is well formed.

```
import sys
from xml.sax.handler import ContentHandler
import xml.sax

fileList = ["emails.xml", "bad.xml"]

#Create a parser object
xmlparser = xml.sax.make_parser()

#Attach a generic content handler to parser
xmlparser.setContentHandler(ContentHandler())

#Parse the files and handle exceptions
#on bad-formed XML files
for fName in fileList:
    try:
        xmlparser.parse(fName)
        print "%s is a well-formed file." % fName
    except Exception, err:
print "ERROR %s:\n\t %s is not a well-formed file."
%
 (err, fName)
```

xml_wellformed.py

```
emails.xml is a well-formed file.
ERROR bad.xml:5:12: not well-formed (invalid token):
        bad.xml is not a well-formed file.
```

Output from xml_wellformed.py code

Accessing Child Nodes

```python
from xml.dom import minidom
xmldoc = minidom.parse('emails.xml')
cNodes = xmldoc.childNodes
#Direct Node Access
print cNodes[0].toxml()
#Find node by name
nList = cNodes[1].getElementsByTagName("to")
#Walk node tree
for node in nList:
    eList = node.getElementsByTagName("addr")
. . .
def printNodes (nList, level):
    for node in nList:
        print ("  ")*level, node.nodeName, \
                node.nodeValue
        printNodes(node.childNodes, level+1)

printNodes(xmldoc.childNodes, 0)
```

Accessing child nodes in a parsed DOM tree can be managed in several different ways. This phrase discusses how to access them using a direct reference, looking up the object by tag name and simply walking the DOM tree.

The first step is to parse the XML document using the minidom.parse(*file*) function to create a DOM tree object. The child nodes of the DOM tree can be accessed directly using the childNodes attribute, which is a list of the child nodes at the root of the tree.

Because the childNodes attribute is a list, nodes can be accessed directly using the following syntax: childNodes[*index*].

NOTE: The first node in the childNodes list of the DOM tree object will be the DTD node.

To search for nodes by their tag name, use the getElementsByTagName(*tag*) of the node object. The getElementsByTagName function accepts a string representation of the tag name for child nodes and returns a list of all child nodes with that tag.

You can also walk the DOM tree recursively by defining a recursive function that will accept a node list; then, call that function and pass the childNodes attribute of the DOM tree object. Finally, recursively call the function again with the childNodes attribute of each child node in the node list, as shown in the sample phrase.

```
from xml.dom import minidom

#Parse XML file to DOM tree
xmldoc = minidom.parse('emails.xml')

#Get nodes at root of tree
cNodes = xmldoc.childNodes

#Direct Node Access
print "DTD Node\n=================="
print cNodes[0].toxml()

#Find node by name
print "\nTo Addresses\n===================="
nList = cNodes[1].getElementsByTagName("to")
for node in nList:
    eList = node.getElementsByTagName("addr")
    for e in eList:
        print e.toxml()

print "\nFrom Addresses\n===================="
nList = cNodes[1].getElementsByTagName("from")
for node in nList:
    eList = node.getElementsByTagName("addr")
```

```
    for e in eList:
        print e.toxml()

#Walk node tree
def printNodes (nList, level):
    for node in nList:
        print ("  ")*level, node.nodeName, \
                node.nodeValue
        printNodes(node.childNodes, level+1)

print "\nNodes\n===================="
printNodes(xmldoc.childNodes, 0)
```

xml_child.py

```
DTD Node
=================
<!DOCTYPE emails [
        <!ELEMENT email (to, from, subject, date,
body)>
        <!ELEMENT to (addr+)>
        <!ELEMENT from (addr)>
        <!ELEMENT subject (#PCDATA)>
        <!ELEMENT date (#PCDATA)>
        <!ELEMENT body (#PCDATA)>
        <!ELEMENT addr (#PCDATA)>
        <!ATTLIST addr type (FROM | TO | CC | BC)
"none">
    ]>

To Addresses
=================
<addr type="TO">bwdayley@novell.com</addr>
<addr type="CC">bwdayley@sfcn.org</addr>
<addr type="TO">bwdayley@novell.com</addr>
<addr type="BC">bwdayley@sfcn.org</addr>

From Addresses
```

```
==================
<addr type="FROM">ddayley@sfcn.org</addr>
<addr type="FROM">cdayley@sfcn.org</addr>

Nodes
==================
 emails None
 emails None
   #text
   email None
     #text
     to None
       #text
       addr None
         #text bwdayley@novell.com
       #text
       addr None
         #text bwdayley@sfcn.org
       #text
     #text
     from None
       #text
       addr None
         #text ddayley@sfcn.org
       #text
     #text
     subject None
       #text
         Update List
     #text
     body None
       #text
         Please add me to the list.
     #text
   #text
. . .
```

Output from xml_child.py code

Accessing Element Attributes

```python
from xml.dom import minidom
xmldoc = minidom.parse('emails.xml')
cNodes = xmldoc.childNodes
print "\nTo Addresses\n===================="
nList = cNodes[1].getElementsByTagName("to")
for node in nList:
    eList = node.getElementsByTagName("addr")
    for e in eList:
        if e.hasAttribute("type"):
            if e.getAttribute("type") == "TO":
                print e.toxml()
```

The first step to accessing element attributes in a XML file is to parse the XML document using the minidom.parse(*file*) function to create a DOM tree object. The child nodes of the DOM tree can be accessed directly using the childNodes attribute, which is a list of the child nodes at the root of the tree.

Use the childNodes attribute to navigate the DOM tree, or search for the elements by their tag name, as described in the previous task, to find the nodes you are looking for.

Once you have found the node, determine whether the node does have the attribute by calling the hasAttribute(*name*) function of the node object, which returns true if the node does contain the attribute specified by name. If the node does have the attribute, you can use the getAttribute(*name*) function to retrieve a string representation of the attribute value.

```python
from xml.dom import minidom

#Parse XML file to DOM tree
xmldoc = minidom.parse('emails.xml')

#Get nodes at root of tree
```

```
cNodes = xmldoc.childNodes

#Find attributes by name
print "\nTo Addresses\n==================="
nList = cNodes[1].getElementsByTagName("to")
for node in nList:
    eList = node.getElementsByTagName("addr")
    for e in eList:
        if e.hasAttribute("type"):
            if e.getAttribute("type") == "TO":
                print e.toxml()

print "\nCC Addresses\n==================="
nList = cNodes[1].getElementsByTagName("to")
for node in nList:
    eList = node.getElementsByTagName("addr")
    for e in eList:
        if e.hasAttribute("type"):
            if e.getAttribute("type") == "CC":
                print e.toxml()

print "\nBC Addresses\n==================="
nList = cNodes[1].getElementsByTagName("to")
for node in nList:
    eList = node.getElementsByTagName("addr")
    for e in eList:
        if e.hasAttribute("type"):
            if e.getAttribute("type") == "BC":
                print e.toxml()
```

xml_attribute.py

```
To Addresses
===================
<addr type="TO">bwdayley@novell.com</addr>
<addr type="TO">bwdayley@novell.com</addr>

CC Addresses
```

```
==================
<addr type="CC">bwdayley@sfcn.org</addr>

BC Addresses

==================
<addr type="BC">bwdayley@sfcn.org</addr>
```

Output from xml_attribute.py code

Adding a Node to a DOM Tree

```
from xml.dom import minidom
DOMimpl = minidom.getDOMImplementation()
xmldoc = DOMimpl.createDocument(None,
"Workstations", None)
doc_root = xmldoc.documentElement
node = xmldoc.createElement("Computer")
doc_root.appendChild(node)
```

Adding child nodes to a DOM tree can be managed in several different ways. This phrase discusses using the xml.dom.minidom module provided with Python to create a DOM tree and add nodes to it.

The first step is to create a DOM object by calling the minidom.getDOMImplementation() function, which returns a DOMImplementation object. Then call the createDocument(*qualifiedName*, *publicId*, *systemId*) function of the DOMImplementation object to create the XML document. The createDocument function returns a Document object.

Once you have created the Document object, create nodes using the createElement(*tagName*) function of the Document object. The createElement function of the Docmuent object returns a node object.

After you have created child nodes, the DOM tree can be constructed using the appendChild(*node*) function to add node objects as child nodes of other node objects. Once the tree has been constructed, add the tree to the Document object using the appendChild(*node*) function of the Document object to attach the topmost level of the tree.

```
from xml.dom import minidom

Station1 = ['Pentium M', '512MB']
Station2 = ['Pentium Core 2', '1024MB']
Station3 = ['Pentium Core Duo', '1024MB']
StationList = [Station1, Station2, Station3]

#Create DOM object
DOMimpl = minidom.getDOMImplementation()

#Create Document
xmldoc = DOMimpl.createDocument(None,
"Workstations", None)
doc_root = xmldoc.documentElement

#Add Nodes
for station in StationList:
    #Create Node
    node = xmldoc.createElement("Computer")

    element = xmldoc.createElement('Processor')
    element.appendChild(xmldoc.createTextNode
(station[0]))
    node.appendChild(element)

    element = xmldoc.createElement('Memory')
    element.appendChild(xmldoc.createTextNode
(station[1]))
```

```
    node.appendChild(element)

    #Add Node
    doc_root.appendChild(node)

print "\nNodes\n==================="
nodeList = doc_root.childNodes
for node in nodeList:
    print node.toprettyxml()

#Write the document
file = open("stations.xml", 'w')
file.write(xmldoc.toxml())
```

xml_addnode.py

```
Nodes
===================
<Computer>
    <Processor>
        Pentium M
    </Processor>
    <Memory>
        512MB
    </Memory>
</Computer>

<Computer>
    <Processor>
        Pentium Core 2
    </Processor>
    <Memory>
        1024MB
    </Memory>
</Computer>

<Computer>
```

```
    <Processor>
        Pentium Core Duo
    </Processor>
    <Memory>
        1024MB
    </Memory>
</Computer>
```

Output from xml_addnode.py code

Removing a Node from a DOM Tree

```
from xml.dom import minidom
xmldoc = minidom.parse('stations.xml')
doc_root = xmldoc.documentElement

doc_root.removeChild(doc_root.childNodes[0])
```

The simplest way to remove a node from a DOM tree is to delete it using a direct reference. The first step is to parse the XML document using the minidom.parse(*file*) function to create a DOM tree document object.

After you have created the document objects, you retrieve the root of the document elements by accessing the documentElement attribute of the document object. To remove an object from the root of the document, use the removeChild(*node*). The removeChild function removes the node and any child nodes from the document.

The child nodes can be referenced directly by using the childNodes attribute of the root or node object. The childNodes attribute is a list, so individual elements can be accessed by their index number as shown in xml_removenode.py.

```
from xml.dom import minidom

#Parse XML file to DOM tree
xmldoc = minidom.parse('stations.xml')
doc_root = xmldoc.documentElement

print "\nNodes\n=================="
nodeList = xmldoc.childNodes
for node in nodeList:
    print node.toprettyxml()

#Delete first node
doc_root.removeChild(doc_root.childNodes[0])

print "\nNodes\n=================="
nodeList = xmldoc.childNodes
for node in nodeList:
    print node.toprettyxml()
```

xml_removenode.py

```
Nodes
==================
<Workstations>
    <Computer>
        <Processor>
            Pentium M
        </Processor>
        <Memory>
            512MB
        </Memory>
    </Computer>
    <Computer>
        <Processor>
            Pentium Core 2
        </Processor>
        <Memory>
```

```
            1024MB
        </Memory>
    </Computer>
    <Computer>
        <Processor>
            Pentium Core Duo
        </Processor>
        <Memory>
            1024MB
        </Memory>
    </Computer>
</Workstations>
Nodes
===================
<Workstations>
    <Computer>
        <Processor>
            Pentium Core 2
        </Processor>
        <Memory>
            1024MB
        </Memory>
    </Computer>
    <Computer>
        <Processor>
            Pentium Core Duo
        </Processor>
        <Memory>
            1024MB
        </Memory>
    </Computer>
</Workstations>
```

Output from xml_removenode.py code

Searching XML Documents

```python
from xml.parsers import expat
class xmlSearch(object):
    def __init__ (self, cStr, nodeName):
        self.nodeName = nodeName
        self.curNode = 0
        self.nodeActive = 0
        self.hits = []
        self.cStr = cStr
    def StartElement(self, name, attributes):
    def EndElement(self, name):
    def CharacterData(self, data):
    def Parse(self, fName):
        xmlParser = expat.ParserCreate()
        xmlParser.StartElementHandler = \
            self.StartElement
        xmlParser.EndElementHandler =
self.EndElement
        xmlParser.CharacterDataHandler = \
                self.CharacterData
        xmlParser.Parse(open(fName).read(), 1)

search = xmlSearch(searchString, searchElement)
search.Parse(xmlFile)
print search.hits
```

Another extremely useful Python module for XML
processing is the xml.parsers.expat module. The expat
module provides an interface to the expat nonvalidat-
ing XML parser. The expat XML parser is a fast parser
that quickly parses XML files and uses handlers to
process character data and markup.

To use the expat parser to quickly search through an
XML document and find specific data, define a search
class that derived from the basic object class.

When the search class is defined, add startElement,
endElement, and CharacterData method that can be
used to override the handlers in the expat parser later.

After you have defined the handler methods of the
search object, define a parse routine that creates the

expat parser by calling the `ParserCreate()` function of the expat module. The `ParserCreate()` function returns an expat parser object.

After the expat parser object is created in the search object's parse routine, override the `StartElementHandler`, `EndElementHandler`, and `CharacterDataHandler` attributes of the parser object by assigning them to the corresponding methods in your search object.

After you have overridden the handler functions of the expat parser object, the parse routine will need to invoke the `Parse(buffer [, isFinal])` function of the expat parser object. The `Parse` function accepts a string *buffer* and parses it using the overridden handler methods.

NOTE: The `isFinal` argument is set to 1 if this is the last data to be parsed or 0 if there is more data to be parsed.

After you have defined the search class, create an instance of the class and use the `Parse` function you defined to parse the XML file and search for data.

```python
from xml.parsers import expat

searchStringList = ["dayley@sfcn.org", "also"]
searchElement = "email"
xmlFile = "emails.xml"

#Define a search class that will handle
#elements and search character data
class xmlSearch(object):
    def __init__ (self, cStr, nodeName):
        self.nodeName = nodeName
        self.curNode = 0
```

```python
        self.nodeActive = 0
        self.hits = []
        self.cStr = cStr
    def StartElement(self, name, attributes):
        if name == self.nodeName:
            self.nodeActive = 1
            self.curNode += 1
    def EndElement(self, name):
        if name == self.nodeName:
            self.nodeActive = 0
    def CharacterData(self, data):
        if data.strip():
            data = data.encode('ascii')
            if self.nodeActive:
                if data.find(self.cStr) != -1:
                    if not
self.hits.count(self.curNode):
                        self.hits.append(self.curNode)
                        print "\tFound %s..." % self.cStr
    def Parse(self, fName):
#Create the expat parser object
        xmlParser = expat.ParserCreate()
#Override the handler methods
        xmlParser.StartElementHandler = \
            self.StartElement
        xmlParser.EndElementHandler =
self.EndElement
        xmlParser.CharacterDataHandler = \
            self.CharacterData
#Parse the XML file
        xmlParser.Parse(open(fName).read(), 1)

for searchString in searchStringList:
#Create search class
    search = xmlSearch(searchString, searchElement)

#Invoke the search objects Parse method
```

```
    print "\nSearching <%s> nodes . . ." % \
            searchElement
    search.Parse(xmlFile)

#Display parsed results
    print "Found '%s' in the following nodes:" % \
            searchString
    print search.hits
```

xml_search.py

```
Searching <email> nodes . . .
    Found dayley@sfcn.org...
    Found dayley@sfcn.org...
Found 'dayley@sfcn.org' in the following nodes:
[1, 2]

Searching <email> nodes . . .
    Found also...
Found 'also' in the following nodes:
[2]
```

Output from xml_search.py code

Extracting Text from XML Documents

```
from xml.parsers import expat
#Define a class that will store the character data
class xmlText(object):
    def __init__ (self):
        self.textBuff = ""
    def CharacterData(self, data):
        data = data.strip()
        if data:
            data = data.encode('ascii')
```

```
            self.textBuff += data + "\n"
    def Parse(self, fName):
        xmlParser = expat.ParserCreate()
    xmlParser.CharacterDataHandler =
self.CharacterData
        xmlParser.Parse(open(fName).read(), 1)

xText = xmlText()
xText.Parse(xmlFile)
print xText.textBuff
```

A common task when parsing XML documents is to quickly retrieve the text from them without the markup tags and attribute data. The expat parser provided with Python provides a simple interface to manage just that. To use the expat parser to quickly parse through an XML document and store only the text, define a simple text parser class that derived from the basic object class.

When the text parser class is defined, add a CharacterData() method that can be used to override the CharacterDataHandlers() method of the expat parser. This method will store the text data passed to the handler when the document is parsed.

After you have defined the handler method of the text parser object, define a parse routine that creates the expat parser by calling the ParserCreate() function of the expat module. The ParserCreate() function returns an expat parser object.

After the expat parser object is created in the text parser object's parse routine, override the CharacterDataHandler attribute of the parser object by assigning it to the CharacterData() method in your search object.

After you have overridden the handler function of the expat parser object, the parse routine will need to invoke the Parse(*buffer* [, *isFinal*]) function of the expat parser object. The Parse function accepts a string *buffer* and parses it using the overridden handler methods.

After you have defined the text parser class, create an instance of the class and use the Parse(*file*) function you defined to parse the XML file and retrieve the text.

```python
from xml.parsers import expat

xmlFile = "emails.xml"

#Define a class that will store the character data
class xmlText(object):
    def __init__ (self):
        self.textBuff = ""
    def CharacterData(self, data):
        data = data.strip()
        if data:
            data = data.encode('ascii')
            self.textBuff += data + "\n"

    def Parse(self, fName):
#Create the expat parser object
        xmlParser = expat.ParserCreate()
#Override the handler methods
        xmlParser.CharacterDataHandler = \
            self.CharacterData
#Parse the XML file
        xmlParser.Parse(open(fName).read(), 1)

#Create the text parser object
xText = xmlText()

#Invoke the text parser objects Parse method
xText.Parse(xmlFile)

#Display parsed results
print "Text from %s\n=====================" % xmlFile
print xText.textBuff
```

xml_text.py

```
Text from emails.xml
==========================
bwdayley@novell.com
bwdayley@sfcn.org
ddayley@sfcn.org
Update List
Please add me to the list.
bwdayley@novell.com
bwdayley@sfcn.org
cdayley@sfcn.org
More Updated List
Please add me to the list also.
```

Output from xml_text.py code

Parsing XML Tags

```
import xml.sax
class tagHandler(xml.sax.handler.ContentHandler):
    def __init__(self):
        self.tags = {}
    def startElement(self,name, attr):
        name = name.encode('ascii')
        self.tags[name] = self.tags.get(name, 0) + 1
        print "Tag %s = %d" % \
                (name, self.tags.get(name))

xmlparser = xml.sax.make_parser()
tHandler = tagHandler()
xmlparser.setContentHandler(tHandler)
xmlparser.parse(xmlFile)
```

Another fairly common task when processing XML files is to process the XML tags themselves. The xml.sax module provides a quick, clean interface to the XML tags by defining a custom content handler to deal with the tags.

This phrase demonstrates how to override the content handler of a sax XML parser to determine how many instances of a specific tag there are in the XML document.

First, define a tag handler class that inherits from the xml.sax.handler.ContentHandler class. Then override the startElement() method of the class to keep track of each encounter with specific tags.

After you have defined the tag handler class, create an xml.sax parser object using the make_parser() function. The make_parser() function will return a parser object that can be used to parse the XML file. Next, create an instance of the tag handler object.

After you have created the parser and tag handler objects, add the custom tag handler object to the parser object using the setContentHandler(handler) function.

After the content handler has been added to the parser object, parse the XML file using the parse(file) command of the parser object.

```python
import xml.sax

xmlFile = "emails.xml"
xmlTag = "email"

#Define handler to scan XML file and parse tags
class tagHandler(xml.sax.handler.ContentHandler):
    def __init__(self):
        self.tags = {}
    def startElement(self,name, attr):
        name = name.encode('ascii')
        self.tags[name] = self.tags.get(name, 0) + 1
        print "Tag %s = %d" % \
                (name, self.tags.get(name))

#Create a parser object
```

```
xmlparser = xml.sax.make_parser()

#Create a content handler object
tHandler = tagHandler()

#Attach the content handler to the parser
xmlparser.setContentHandler(tHandler)

#Parse the XML file
xmlparser.parse(xmlFile)
tags = tHandler.tags
if tags.has_key(xmlTag):
    print "%s has %d <%s> nodes." % \
          (xmlFile, tags[xmlTag], xmlTag)
```

xml_tags.py

```
Tag emails = 1
Tag email = 1
Tag to = 1
Tag addr = 1
Tag addr = 2
Tag from = 1
Tag addr = 3
Tag subject = 1
Tag body = 1
Tag email = 2
Tag to = 2
Tag addr = 4
Tag addr = 5
Tag from = 2
Tag addr = 6
Tag subject = 2
Tag body = 2
emails.xml has 2 <email> nodes.
```

Output from xml_tags.py code

Programming Web Services

The Python language has an excellent set of modules to handle various web service needs. The phrases in this chapter are designed to give you a quick insight into some of the more useful and common ways in which Python can be used to program web services.

The first set of phrases show how to write CGI scripts using the Python language to send HTML to web browsers, handle form requests, and send posts to themselves, as well as allow users to upload files to the server via the web browser.

The next set of phrases provide examples of using Python to create web servers to handle GET and POST requests, as well as creating a simple CGI script server.

The final two phrases show how to use Python to create HTTP client connections to web servers to send POST and GET requests and then handle the response back from the web server.

Adding HTML to Web Pages Using CGI Scripts

```
#!/usr/bin/python
print "Content-type: text/html\n"
print "<title>CGI Text</title>\n"
webText = """
<H1>Useful Python Links</H1>
. . .
"""
print webText
```

Adding HTML content to web pages using Python CGI scripts is a very straightforward and simple process. The first line of the CGI script should be nonexecutable and point to the location of the Python interpreter using the #!<path> syntax.

When the CGI script is called by the web server, all output to stdout is directed back to the web browser. All you need to do to send the HTML code to the browser is print it to stdout.

NOTE: The permission on the CGI scripts must be executable. You will need to set the file permission to 755 on Linux servers for the scripts to be able to execute.

NOTE: Scripts that are created with the DOS EOL character set \r\n will not run properly on Linux web servers.

Depending on the web server you are using, you might need to make configuration changes to understand how to serve CGI files.

```
#!/usr/bin/python

#Send header to browser
print "Content-type: text/html\n"
print "<title>CGI Text</title>\n"

webText = """
<H1>Useful Python Links</H1>
<li><a href="http://www.python.org">
Python Web Site</a></li>
<li><a href="http://docs.python.org">
Python Documentation</a></li>
<li><a href="http://cheeseshop.python.org">
Cheeseshop (Python Packages Library)</a></li>
"""

#Send page content to browser
print webText
```

cgi_text.cgi

```
<!DOCTYPE html>
<html lang="en" xml:lang="en">
<head>
<meta content="text/html; charset=utf-8"
 http-equiv="content-type" />
<title>Form Page</title>
</head>
<body>
<H1>Test Link to CGI Script</H1>
<A HREF="cgi_text.cgi">cgi_text.cgi</A></body>
</html>
```

cgi_link.html

Figure 10.1 shows how cgi_text.cgi appears in a web browser.

Figure 10.1   Output HTML page created by cgi_text.cgi code.

Processing Parameters Passed to CGI Scripts

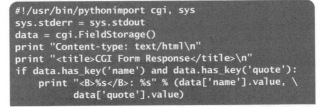

```
#!/usr/bin/pythonimport cgi, sys
sys.stderr = sys.stdout
data = cgi.FieldStorage()
print "Content-type: text/html\n"
print "<title>CGI Form Response</title>\n"
if data.has_key('name') and data.has_key('quote'):
    print "<B>%s</B>: %s" % (data['name'].value, \
          data['quote'].value)
```

The cgi module included with Python provides basic access to the metadata that gets passed to the CGI script when it is executed. When writing a CGI script that needs to accept parameters, use the `cgi.FieldStorage()` function to parse the fields sent in the POST or GET request to the web server. `FieldStorage` returns a dictionary of fields that were included with the request.

Parameters can be accessed from the dictionary returned by `FieldStorage` by using the standard Python syntax to access the keys and values of the dictionary. In the example, `has_key(key)` is used to determine whether a key exists, and then the value is directly accessed using the `d[key].value` syntax.

NOTE: Parameters can be passed to CGI scripts through either a POST or a GET request. The example illustrates how to use a HTML form to send a POST request and a direct link to send a GET request.

```python
#!/usr/bin/pythonimport cgi, sys

#Send errors to browser
sys.stderr = sys.stdout

#Parse data from form
data = cgi.FieldStorage()

#Send response to browser
print "Content-type: text/html\n"
print "<title>CGI Form Response</title>\n"
print "<h2>Current Quote</h2><P>"

if data.has_key('name') and data.has_key('quote'):
    print "<B>%s</B>: %s" % (data['name'].value, \
          data['quote'].value)
```

cgi_form.py

```html
<!DOCTYPE html>
<html lang="en">
<head>
<meta content="text/html; charset=utf-8"
 http-equiv="content-type" />
<title>Form Page</title>
</head>
<body>
<h2>Form Post</h2><p>
<form method="POST" action="/cgi_form.cgi">
    Name <input type="TEXT" name="name">
    <P>
```

```
    Quote <input type="TEXT" name="quote" size="80">
    <P>
    <input type="SUBMIT" value="send">
</form><p>
<h2>Direct Links</h2><p>
<li><a href="cgi_form.cgi?
name=Brad&quote=G'Day!">G'Day!</a>
<li><a href="cgi_form.cgi?
name=Brad&quote=Bad Show!">Bad Show!</a>
</body>
</html>
```

form.html

Figure 10.2 shows form.html loaded in a web browser.

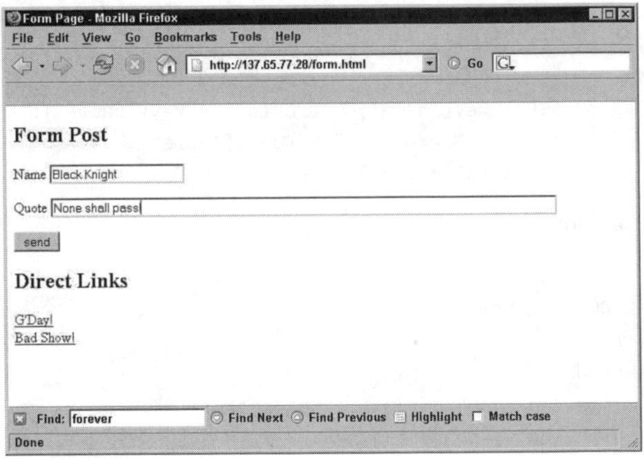

Figure 10.2   Web browser view of form.html code.

Figure 10.3 shows the web page created when form.html executes cgi_form.cgi.

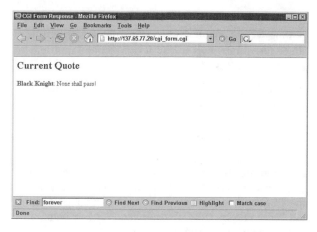

Figure 10.3   Output HTML page created by cgi_form.cgi code.

Creating Self-Posting CGI Scripts

```
#!/usr/bin/pythonimport cgi, os, sys
data = cgi.FieldStorage()
formText = """Content-type: text/html\n
<form method="POST" action="cgi_selfpost.cgi">
    Name <input type="TEXT" name="name">
    Quote <input type="TEXT" name="quote" size="80">
    <input type="SUBMIT" value="send">
</FORM>
"""
print formText
if data.has_key('name') and data.has_key('quote'):
    f = open("quotes.dat", 'a')
    f.write("<li><b>%s:</b> %s</li>\n" % \
            (data['name'].value,
data['quote'].value))
    f=open("quotes.dat", 'r')
if f:
    print f.read()
```

A *self-posting* CGI script is one that posts to itself. Self-posting scripts enable you to keep all your code in a single file rather than spread it out through multiple HTML and CGI files.

In addition to the first line, you will need to add code to parse the data from the CGI posts, handle the parameters from the CGI post, and write forms to the web browser that posts the CGI script.

NOTE: In the example, the self-posting form is added to the script even if no parameters are passed when the CGI script is loaded. However, the initial posting to the script can be from another script or web page, as well as a self-post from the same script.

Typically, you will want to parse the data and handle arguments first because most self-posting CGI scripts will write different views back to the web browser depending on what parameters were posted.

The CGI post data can be parsed using the `cgi.FieldStorage()` function. `FieldStorage` returns a dictionary of fields that were included with the request.

Parameters can be accessed from the dictionary returned by `FieldStorage` by using the standard Python syntax to access the keys and values of the dictionary. In the example, `has_key(key)` is used to determine whether a key exists, and then the value is directly accessed using the `d[key].value` syntax.

After you have accessed the parameters, you can use their values to determine what HTML view needs to be sent back to the web browser through stdout, which writes back to the web browser.

NOTE: Each time a post is received, the CGI script is reloaded. No local or global data is retained. If you need to have data survive between multiple posts, you will need to store it locally on the server. In the following example, the quotes are captured and stored in a local data file on the server so that they can be displayed each time a new post is received.

```python
import cgi, os, sys

#Send errors to browser
sys.stderr = sys.stdout

#Parse data from form
data = cgi.FieldStorage()

#Send form to browser
formText = """Content-type: text/html\n
<title>CGI Self-Post Form</title>\n
<h2>Enter Quote</h2><P>
<form method="POST" action="cgi_selfpost.cgi">
    Name <input type="TEXT" name="name">
    <p>
    Quote <input type="TEXT" name="quote" size="80">
    <p>
    <input type="SUBMIT" value="send">
</form>
<hr>
<h2>Received Quotes</h2><p>"""
print formText

#Retrieve field from form and store data
if data.has_key('name') and data.has_key('quote'):
    f = open("quotes.dat", 'a')
    f.write("<li><b>%s:</b> %s</li>\n" % \
            (data['name'].value,
data['quote'].value))
    f.close()
```

```
#Send stored data to browser
f=open("quotes.dat", 'r')
if f:
    print f.read()
    f.close()
```

cgi_selfpost.cgi

```
<LI><B>King Arthur:</B> I am your king!</LI>
<LI><B>Peasant:</B> I didn't vote for you.</LI>
<LI><B>King Arthur:
</B> You don't vote for a king!</LI>
<LI><B>Black Knight:</B> None shall pass!</LI>
<LI><B>Bridge Keeper:
</B> What is the air speed velocity of
 an unlaiden swallow?</LI>
```

Contents of quotes.dat data file

Figure 10.4 displays the web page that cgi_selfpost.cgi generates as items are posted to it.

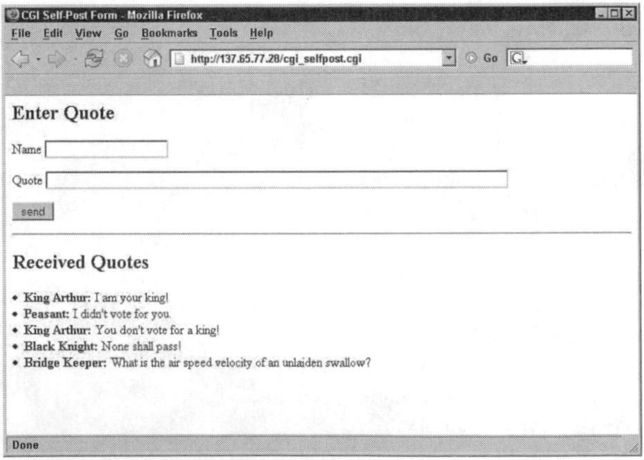

Figure 10.4   Web browser view of cgi_selfpost.cgi.

Allowing Users to Upload Files via CGI Scripts

```
#!/usr/bin/pythonimport cgi, os, sys, string
import posixpath, macpath
data = cgi.FieldStorage()
if data.has_key('uFile'):
    saveFile(data['uFile'])
    print "<B>%s</B> uploaded (%d bytes)." \
        % (data['uFile'].filename, bytes)
```

A common task when programming web services is allowing users to upload files to the server using the web browser. This is fairly easy to accomplish with Python CGI scripts. First, create an HTML page that includes a form with a type=file INPUT tag. The name attribute of the INPUT tag will be used by the CGI script to retrieve the file information. The form should specify your Python CGI script as the action. The enctype attribute of the form element must be set to multipart/form-data.

Once you have built the HTML file, create a Python script that will parse the parameters from the POST request using the cgi.FieldStorage() function. FieldStorage() returns a dictionary of fields passed to the CGI script.

Using the dictionary returned by FieldStorage() should include the key you specified as the name of the INPUT tag in the HTML document. Use that key to obtain the file information object. The filename can be accessed by using the filename attribute of the object, and the actual data can be accessed using the file attribute. The file attribute acts similar to a read-only file that you can read using read(), readline(), or readlines().

Read the file contents from the file object and write it to a file on the server.

NOTE: In the example, the entire file was read at once. For larger files, you might want to break up the read into segments to reduce the load on the system.

NOTE: It might be a good idea in practical terms to filter the pathname to remove restricted characters and characters that might alter the path.

```python
#!/usr/bin/pythonimport cgi, os, sys, string
import posixpath, macpath

saveDir = "/upload"

#Send errors to browser
sys.stderr = sys.stdout

#Parse data from form
data = cgi.FieldStorage()

#Save the file to server directory
def saveFile(uFile):
    fPath = "%s/%s" % (saveDir, uFile.filename)
    buf = uFile.file.read()
    bytes = len(buf)
    sFile = open(fPath, 'wb')
    sFile.write(buf)
    sFile.close()


#Send response to browser
webText = """Content-type: text/html\n"
```

```
<title>CGI Upload Form</title>\n
<h2>Upload File</h2><p>"""
print webText

if data.has_key('uFile'):
    saveFile(data['uFile'])
    print "<b>%s</b> uploaded (%d bytes)." % \
          (data['uFile'].filename, bytes)
```

cgi_upload.cgi

```
<!DOCTYPE html>
<html lang="en">
<head>
<meta content="text/html; charset=utf-8"
 http-equiv="content-type" />
<title>Upload Form Page</title>
</head>
<body>
<h2>Upload File</h2><P>
<form enctype="multipart/form-data" method="POST"
 action="cgi_upload.cgi">
    <input type="file" size="70" name="uFile">
    <p><input type="SUBMIT" value="upload">
</form>
</body>
</html>
```

upload.html

Figure 10.5 shows upload.html loaded in a web browser.

Figure 10.6 shows the web page generated by cgi_upload.cgi when the upload action is performed by form.html.

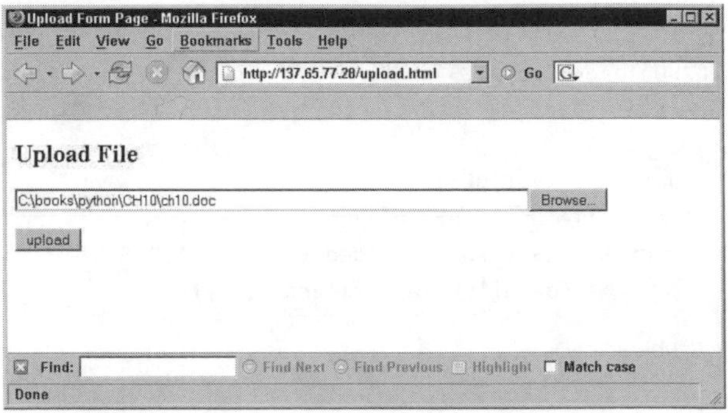

Figure 10.5   Web browser view of upload.html code.

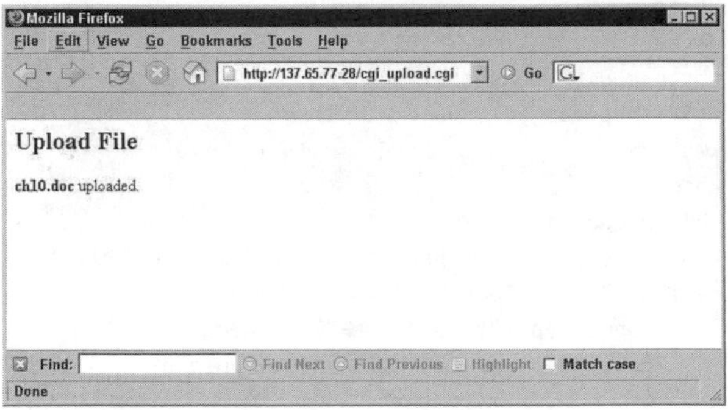

Figure 10.6   Output HTML page created by
cgi_upload.cgi code.

Creating an HTTP Server to Handle GET Requests

```
import BaseHTTPServer, cgi
class httpServHandler \
    (BaseHTTPServer.BaseHTTPRequestHandler):
    def do_GET(self):
```

```
        if self.path.find('?') != -1:
            self.path, self.query_string = \
                self.path.split('?', 1)
        else:
            self.query_string = ''
        self.send_response(200)
        self.send_header('Content-type',
'text/html')
        self.end_headers()
        self.globals = \
            dict(cgi.parse_qsl(self.query_string))
        sys.stdout = self.wfile
        self.wfile.write("<H2>Handle Get</H2><P>")
        self.wfile.write( \
            "<LI>Executing <B>%s</B>" % (self.path))
        self.wfile.write( \
            "<LI>With Globals<B>%s</B><HR>" % \
            (self.globals))
        execfile(self.path, self.globals)

os.chdir('/myTest')
serv = BaseHTTPServer.HTTPServer( \
            servAddr, httpServHandler)
serv.serve_forever()
```

A very common task when programming web services
is to create web servers to handle special processing of
GET requests from web browsers. The
BaseHTTPServer module included with Python provides a set of classes and functions that allow you to
create custom web servers to handle these requests.
The first step is to define a handler class derived from
the BaseHTTPServer.BaseHTTPRequestHandler class that
overrides the do_GET() method.

Inside the do_GET method, you can use the path attribute to get the file path the GET request was directed
toward. The path attribute includes the entire string of
the GET request, including the path and parameters in
the format path?*param=value&param=value*.... If there
were parameters passed in the GET request, they can
be parsed out by using the split('?') function on the

path string to split it into a path and query string, as illustrated by the sample code http_get_serv.py.

When you have the query string of the POST request in a buffer, use `cgi.parse_qsl(string)` to parse the query string into a dictionary, as shown in the example http_get_serv.py. The arguments will be added to the dictionary and can be accessed by using standard Python syntax.

NOTE: In the sample code, we are using the web server to remotely execute a Python script. We redirect the `sys.stdout` to the `wfile` attribute of the handler class so that normal output from the script executing will be displayed in the web browser.

Once you have defined the handler class and overridden the `do_GET` method, create an instance of the web server using `BaseHTTPServer.HTTPServer(address, handler)`. The `address` argument is a list including the server address and port, respectively. The `handler` argument is the custom handler class you defined earlier.

After you have created an instance of the web server, start the web server by calling its `serve_forever()` function.

```python
import os, sys
import BaseHTTPServer, cgi

servAddr = ('',8080)

#Define the HTTP handler that overrides do_GET
class httpServHandler( \
    BaseHTTPServer.BaseHTTPRequestHandler):
    def do_GET(self):
```

```python
        if self.path.find('?') != -1:
            self.path, self.query_string = \
                self.path.split('?', 1)
        else:
            self.query_string = ''
        self.send_response(200)
        self.send_header('Content-type',
'text/html')
        self.end_headers()

#Setup Global Environment
        self.globals = \
            dict(cgi.parse_qsl(self.query_string))
#Redirect output to browser
        sys.stdout = self.wfile

#Execute the script remotely
        self.wfile.write("<h2>Handle Get</h2><P>")
        self.wfile.write(
           "<LI>Executing <b>%s</b>" % (self.path))
        self.wfile.write( \
           "<li>With Globals<B>%s</b><hr>" % \
          (self.globals))
        execfile(self.path, self.globals)

#Set the root directory
os.chdir('/myTest')

#Create server object
serv = BaseHTTPServer.HTTPServer( \
           servAddr, httpServHandler)

#Start Server
serv.serve_forever()
```

http_get_serv.py

```
if name and quote:
    print "<B>%s</B> says <I>%s</I>"% (name, quote)
else:
    print "There were errors in the parameters."
```

http_text.py

Figure 10.7 shows the web page generated by http_get_serv.py when it receives a GET request.

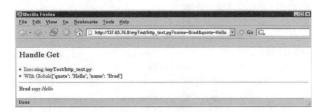

Figure 10.7   Output HTML page created by http_get_serv.py code.

Creating an HTTP Server to Handle POST Requests

```
import BaseHTTPServer, cgi
class httpServHandler( \
      BaseHTTPServer.BaseHTTPRequestHandler):
    def do_POST(self):
        self.query_string = self.rfile.read
(int(self.headers['Content-Length']))
        self.args = dict(cgi.parse_\
                      qsl(self.query_string))
        self.send_response(200)
        self.send_header('Content-type', \
                         'text/html')
        self.end_headers()
        sys.stdout = self.wfile
```

```
        self.wfile.write( \
            "<h2>Handling Post</h2><P>")
        self.wfile.write( \
            "<li>Location: <b>%s</b>"%(self.path))
        self.wfile.write( \
            "<li>Arguments:<b>%s</b><hr>"% \
                            (self.args))
        execfile(self.path, self.args)

serv = BaseHTTPServer.HTTPServer( \
        servAddr, httpServHandler)
serv.serve_forever()
```

A very common task when programming web services is to create web servers to handle special processing of POST requests from web browsers. The BaseHTTPServer module included with Python provides a set of classes and functions that allow you to create custom web servers to handle these requests.

The first step is to define a handler class derived from the `BaseHTTPServer.BaseHTTPRequestHandler` class that overrides the do_POST() method.

The first order of business inside the `do_POST` method is to get the arguments passed with the POST request. First, get the length of the content by accessing the value of the `Content-Length` key in the `headers` attribute of the handler object. When you know the size of the contents, read the query string from the `rfile` attribute into a buffer.

After you have the query string of the POST request in a buffer, use `cgi.parse_qsl(string)` to parse the query string into a dictionary, as shown in the example http_post_serv.py. The arguments will be added to the dictionary and can be accessed by using standard Python syntax.

NOTE: In the sample code, we are using the web server to remotely execute a Python script. We redirect the sys.stdout to the wfile attribute of the handler class so that normal output from the script executing will be displayed in the web browser.

After you have defined the handler class and overridden the do_POST method, create an instance of the web server using BaseHTTPServer.HTTPServer(*address*, *handler*). The *address* argument is a list including the server address and port, respectively. The *handler* argument is the custom handler class you defined earlier.

Once you have created an instance of the web server, start the web server by calling its serve_forever() function.

```
import os, sys
import BaseHTTPServer, cgi

servAddr = ('',80)

#Define the HTTP handler that overrides do_POST
class httpServHandler( \
      BaseHTTPServer.BaseHTTPRequestHandler):
   def do_POST(self):
#Get arguments from query string
        self.query_string = self.rfile.read( \
            int(self.headers['Content-Length']))
        self.args = dict(cgi.parse_ \
                          qsl(self.query_string))

        self.send_response(200)
        self.send_header('Content-type', \
                          'text/html')
        self.end_headers()

#Redirect output to browser
```

```
        sys.stdout = self.wfile

#Handle the post
        self.wfile.write("<h2>Handling \
            Post</h2><P>")
        self.wfile.write("<li>Location: \
            <b>%s</b>"%(self.path))
        self.wfile.write("<li>Arguments: \
            <b>%s</b><hr>"%(self.args))

#Execute the script remotely
        execfile(self.path, self.args)

#Set the root directory
os.chdir('/myTest')

#Create server object
serv = BaseHTTPServer.HTTPServer( \
          servAddr, httpServHandler)

#Start Server
serv.serve_forever()
```

http_post_serv.py

```
<!DOCTYPE html>
<html lang="en">
<head>
<meta content="text/html; charset=utf-8"
http-equiv="content-type" />
<title>Form Page</title>
</head>
<body>
<form method="POST" action=
 "http://testserver.net/myTest/http_text.py">
    Name <input type="TEXT" name="name">
    <p>
```

```
    Quote <input type="TEXT" NAME="quote" size="80">
    <p>
    <input type="SUBMIT" value="send">
</form>
</body>
</html>
```

post_form.html

```
if name and quote:
    print "<b>%s</b> says <i>%s</i>"% (name, quote)
else:
    print "There were errors in the parameters."
```

http_text.py

Figure 10.8 shows post_form.html displayed in a web browser.

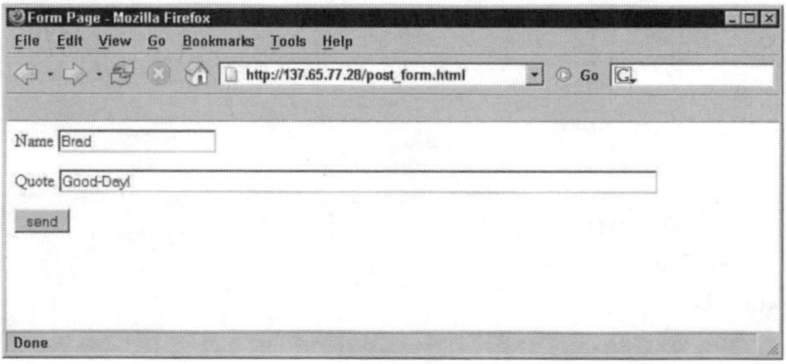

Figure 10.8   Web browser view of post_form.html code.

Figure 10.9 shows the web page generated by http_post_serv.py when it receives a POST request.

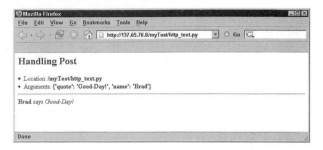

Figure 10.9 Output HTML page created by http_post_serv.py code.

Creating an HTTP Server to Process CGI Scripts

```
import os
import BaseHTTPServer, CGIHTTPServer
serverAddr = ("", 80)
os.chdir("/myTest")
serv = BaseHTTPServer.HTTPServer( \
    serverAddr, CGIHTTPServer.CGIHTTPRequestHandler)
serv.serve_forever()
```

Python includes the CGIHTTPServer module that provides a quick and easy way to create your own CGI script server, eliminating the need to set up and configure a web server. This can be extremely time-saving.

To set up a simple CGI script server, first set the root directory for the server to act in, and then create an instance of the CGI script server using BaseHTTPServer.HTTPServer(*address*, *handler*). The *address* argument is a list including the server address and port, respectively. A simple server handler should specify the default handler of CGIHTTPServer.CGIHTTPRequestHandler. The CGIHTTPRequestHandler is similar to a normal

HTTPRequestHandler; however, the do_GET and do_HEAD
functions have been modified to handle CGI scripts,
and the do_POST method will only allow posting to
CGI scripts.

NOTE: You can override the do_GET, do_HEAD, and
do_POST methods to create a customized CGI script
parser.

After you have created an instance of the CGI script
server, start the server by calling its serve_forever()
function.

NOTE: The default location for CGI scripts is /cgi-bin
or /htbin, relative to the root directory of the script
server. The CGI scripts will need to reside in one of
these two locations, and the Linux permissions must be
set so that the scripts are executable (typically 0755).

```python
import os
import BaseHTTPServer, CGIHTTPServer

serverAddr = ("", 80)

#Set root directory
os.chdir("/myTest")

#Create server object
serv = BaseHTTPServer.HTTPServer( \
    serverAddr, CGIHTTPServer.CGIHTTPRequestHandler)

#Start server
serv.serve_forever()
```

cgi_serv.py

Figure 10.10 shows the web page generated by cgi_form.cgi as it is executed by the cgi_serv.py script.

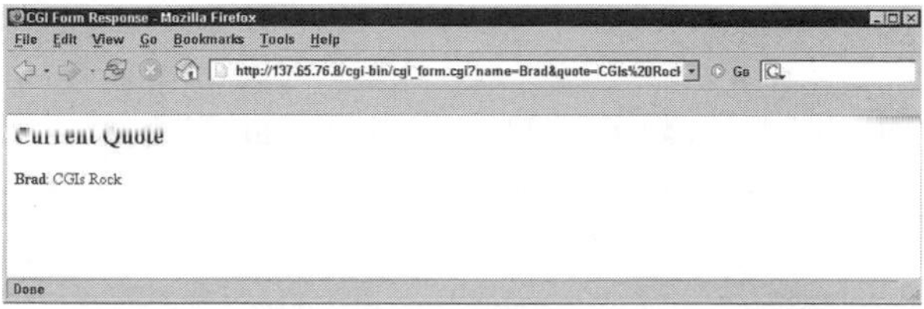

Figure 10.10   Output HTML page created by cgi_form.cgi code executed by cgi_serv.py.

Sending an HTTP GET Request from a Python Script

```python
import httplib
httpServ = \
    httplib.HTTPConnection("testserver.net", 80)
httpServ.connect()

httpServ.request('GET', "/test.html")
response = httpServ.getresponse()
if response.status == httplib.OK:
    printText (response.read())

httpServ.request('GET',
    '/cgi_form.cgi?name=Brad&quote=Testing.')
response = httpServ.getresponse()
if response.status == httplib.OK:
    printText (response.read())
```

Another important task when programming web services is to send GET requests directly to a web server from a Python script rather to than a web browser. This effectively allows you to write client-side applications without having to deal with the web browser.

The httplib module included with Python provides the classes and functions to connect to a web server, send a GET request, and handle the response.

First, create a server connection object by executing the httplib.HTTPConnection(*address, port*) function, which returns an HTTPServer object. Then connect to the server by calling the connect() function of the HTTPServer object.

To send the GET request, call request(*method* [, *url* [, *body* [, *headers*). Specify GET as the method of the request, and then specify the location of the file as the url.

NOTE: In the sample code, we send a CGI script with parameters. Because the web server executed the CGI script, the response from the server will be the output of the CGI script, not the script itself.

After you have sent the request, get the server's response using the getresponse() function of the HTTPServer object. The getresponse() function returns a response object that acts like a file object, allowing you to read the response using the read() request.

NOTE: You can check the status of the response by accessing the status attribute of the response object.

```
import httplib

def printText(txt):
    lines = txt.split('\n')
    for line in lines:
```

```
        print line.strip()

#Connect to server
httpServ = \
   httplib.HTTPConnection("testserver.net", 80)
httpServ.connect()

#Send Get html request
httpServ.request('GET', "/test.html")

#Wait for response
response = httpServ.getresponse()
if response.status == httplib.OK:
    print "Output from HTML request"
    print "==========================="
    printText (response.read())

#Send Get cgi request
httpServ.request('GET', \
    '/cgi_form.cgi?name=Brad&quote=Testing.')

#Wait for response
response = httpServ.getresponse()
if response.status == httplib.OK:
    print "Output from CGI request"
    print "========================="
    printText (response.read())

httpServ.close()
```

http_get.py

```
Output from HTML request
===========================
<!DOCTYPE html>
<html lang="en" xml:lang="en">
<head>
```

```
<meta content="text/html; charset=utf-8"
 http-equiv="content-type" />
<title>HTML Page</title>
</head>
<body>
<h1>Test Link to CGI Script</h1>
<a href="cgi_text.cgi">cgi_text.cgi</A></body>
</html>

Output from CGI request
=========================
<title>CGI Form Response</title>

<h2>Current Quote</h2><p>
<b>Brad</b>: Testing.
```

Output from http_get.py code

Sending an HTTP POST Request from a Python Script

```
import httplib
httpServ = httplib.HTTPConnection("testserver.net",
80)
httpServ.connect()
quote = "Use a Python script to post to the CGI
Script."
httpServ.request('POST', '/cgi_form.cgi',
'name=Brad&quote=%s' \
    % quote)
    response = httpServ.getresponse()
    if response.status == httplib.OK:
    printText (response.read())
httpServ.close()
```

You also might need to send POST requests directly to a web server from a Python script rather than a web browser. This effectively enables you to write client-side applications without having to deal with the web browser.

The httplib module included with Python provides the classes and functions to connect to a web server, send a POST request, and handle the response without the use of a web browser.

First, create a server connection object by executing the `httplib.HTTPConnection(`*address, port*`)` function, which returns an HTTPServer object. Then connect to the server by calling the `connect()` function of the HTTPServer object.

To send the POST request, call `request(`*method* [, *url* [, *body* [, *headers*`)`. Specify POST as the *method* of the request. Specify the location of the script to handle the post as the *url*. Specify the query string that needs to be passed with the POST as the *body*.

NOTE: In the sample code, we send a CGI script with parameters. Because the web server executed the CGI script, the response from the server will be the output of the CGI script, not the script itself.

After you have sent the request, get the server's response using the `getresponse()` function of the HTTPServer object. The `getresponse()` function returns a response object that acts like a file object, allowing you to read the response using the `read()` request.

NOTE: You can check the status of the response by accessing the status attribute of the response object.

```python
import httplib

def printText(txt):
    lines = txt.split('\n')
    for line in lines:
        print line.strip()

#Connect to server
httpServ = httplib.HTTPConnection("testserver.net",
80)
httpServ.connect()

#Send Get cgi request
quote = \
"Use a Python script to post to the CGI Script."
httpServ.request('POST', \
'/cgi_form.cgi', 'name=Brad&quote=%s' % quote)

#Wait for response
response = httpServ.getresponse()
if response.status == httplib.OK:
    print "Output from CGI request"
    print "========================="
    printText (response.read())

httpServ.close()
```

http_post.py

```
Output from CGI request
=========================
<title>CGI Form Response</title>

<h2>Current Quote</h2><P>
<b>Brad</b>:
Use a Python script to post to the CGI Script.
```

Output from http_post.py code

Creating an XML-RPC Server

```
import SimpleXMLRPCServer

serv =
SimpleXMLRPCServer.SimpleXMLRPCServer(servAddr)
serv.register_function(areaSquare)
serv.register_introspection_functions()
serv.serve_forever()
```

The SimpleXMLRPCServer module provided with
Python allows you to implement web services that
support the XML-RPC protocol for remote procedure
calls or RPCs. The XML-RPC protocol uses XML
data encoding to transmit remote procedure calls across
the HTTP protocol. This section discusses how to use
the SimpleXMLRPCServer module to create a simple
XML-RPC server.

The first step is to create an XML-RPC server object
by calling the SimpleXMLRPCServer(*addr* [,
requestHandler [, *logRequests*]]) function of the
SimpleXMLRPCServer module. The SimpleXMLRPCServer
function accepts a list containing the address and port
to use for the server and returns an XML-RPC server
object. The *requstHandler* argument specifies a request
handler object if needed, and the *logRequests* is a
Boolean flag that specifies whether or not to log
incoming requests.

After you have created the XML-RPC server object,
register locally defined functions that will be provided
remotely by calling the register_function(*function*)
function of the XML-RPC server object.

After you have registered the local functions that will
be provided remotely, register the introspection functions using the register_introspection_functions
(*function*) function of the XML-RPC server object.

The XML-RPC server supports the XML introspection API, which provides the system.listMethods(), system.methodHelp(), and system.MethodSignature() introspection functions. The register_introspection _functions() function registers those introspection functions so that they can be accessed by a remote client.

After you have registered the introspection functions, start the server using the serve_forever() function of the XML-RPC server object. The server will begin accepting remote procedure call requests from remote clients.

```python
import SimpleXMLRPCServer

servAddr = ("localhost", 8080)

def areaSquare(length):
    return length*length

def areaRectangle(length, width):
    return length*width

def areaCircle(radius):
    return 3.14*(radius*radius)

serv =
SimpleXMLRPCServer.SimpleXMLRPCServer(servAddr)

#Register RPC functions
serv.register_function(areaSquare)
serv.register_function(areaRectangle)
serv.register_function(areaCircle)

#Register Introspective functions
```

```
serv.register_introspection_functions()

#Handle Requests
serv.serve_forever()
```

xml-rpc_serv.py

Creating an XML-RPC Client

```
import xmlrpclib
servAddr = "http://localhost:8080"
s = xmlrpclib.ServerProxy(servAddr)
methods = s.system.listMethods()
s.areaSquare(5)
s.areaRectangle(4,5)
s.areaCircle(5)
```

The xmlrpclib module provided with Python allows you to create clients that can access web services that support the XML-RPC protocol. The XML-RPC protocol uses XML data encoding to transmit remote procedure calls across the HTTP protocol. This section discusses how to use the xmlrpclib module to create a client to access an XML-RPC server.

The first step is to authenticate to the XML-RPC proxy server by calling the ServerProxy(*uri* [, *transport* [, *encoding* [, *verbose* [, *allow_none*]]]]) function. The ServerProxy function connects to the remote location specified by *uri* and returns an instance of the ServerProxy object.

After you have connected to the XML-RPC server, you can invoke methods on the remote server by calling them as a function of the ServerProject object. For example, you can call the introspection system. listMethods() using the "." syntax shown in the sample

code xml–rpc_client.py. The system.listMethods()
function returns a list of functions that are available on
the XML-RPC server. Other remote functions that are
registered on the XML-RPC server are invoked the
same way.

```python
import xmlrpclib

servAddr = "http://localhost:8080"

#Attach to XML-RPC server
s = xmlrpclib.ServerProxy(servAddr)

#List Methods
print "Methods\n==============="
methods = s.system.listMethods()
for m in methods:
    print m

#Call Methods
print "\nArea\n==============="
print "5 in. Square =", s.areaSquare(5)
print "4x5 in. Rectangle =", s.areaRectangle(4,5)
print "10 in. Circle =", s.areaCircle(5)
```

xml-rpc_client.py

```
Methods
===============
areaCircle
areaRectangle
areaSquare
system.listMethods
system.methodHelp
system.methodSignature

Area
```

```
=================
5 in. Square = 25
4x5 in. Rectangle = 20
10 in. Circle = 78.5
```

Output of xml-rpc_client.py

Using SOAPpy to Access SOAP Web Services Through a WSDL File

```
from SOAPpy import WSDL

wServer = WSDL.Proxy( \
        'http://api.google.com/GoogleSearch.wsdl')
print wServer.methods.keys()

methodData = wServer.methods['doGoogleSearch']
for p in methodData.inparams:
    print "  %s %s" % (p.name.ljust(12), p.type[1])
hits = wServer.doGoogleSearch(key, searchStr, 0, \
        10, False, "", False, "", "utf-8", "utf-8")
print len(hits.resultElements), "Hits . . ."
for hit in hits.resultElements:
    print "\nURL:", hit.URL
    print "Title:", hit.title
    print "Desc:", hit.snippet
```

The dynamics of the Python language make it a perfect fit for SOAP web services. The SOAPpy module, available at http://pywebsvcs.sourceforge.net/, includes functions that enable you to create Python scripts that allow you to access SOAP web services.

This phrase is designed to familiarize you with using the SOAPpy module to access SOAP web services through a Web Service Definition Language (WSDL) file. A WSDL file is an XML file that describes the URL, namespace, type of web service, functions, arguments, argument data types, and function return values of the SOAP web service. In this case, the sample code accesses the Google search SOAP web service through the GoogleSearch.wsdl file.

The first step is to create an instance of the WSDL proxy server using the `WSDL.Proxy(wsdlfile)` function of the SOAPpy module. The `WSDL.Proxy` function accepts a WSDL filename as its only argument and returns a WSDL proxy server object.

After you have created the WSDL proxy server object, you can view the available methods using the `methods` attribute of the WSDL proxy server object, as shown in the sample code `wServer.methods.keys()`. The `methods` attribute is a dictionary containing the available methods of the web service.

To view the arguments associated with a specific method, look up the method in the dictionary to get a method data object, as shown in the sample code `Server.methods['doGoogleSearch']`. Once you have the method data object, the arguments can be accessed using the `inparams` attribute, which is a list of parameter objects. The name and type of the parameter are available using the `name` and `type` attributes of the parameter object, as shown in the sample code `p.name.ljust(12), p.type[1]`.

The methods on the SOAP server can be called as methods of the WSDL proxy server object using the "." syntax as shown in the example soap_wsdl.py.

NOTE: This phrase focuses on using Google's SOAP web service; however, there are numerous services out there that can be accessed in much the same way. A good place to start is to look at the services provided at http://www.xmethods.net/.

NOTE: In the sample code, *key* is set to
INSERT_YOUR_KEY_HERE. You will need to go to
http://api.google.com and create an account to get
your own key. Once you have your own key, insert it
into the sample code.

```python
from SOAPpy import WSDL

searchStr = 'python'
key = 'INSERT_YOUR_KEY_HERE'

#Create WSDL server object
wServer = WSDL.Proxy( \
        'http://api.google.com/GoogleSearch.wsdl')

#Display methods
print "\nAvailable Methods\n====================="
print wServer.methods.keys()

#Display method arguments
print "\ndoGoogleSearch Args\n==================="
methodData = wServer.methods['doGoogleSearch']
for p in methodData.inparams:
    print "  %s %s" % (p.name.ljust(12), p.type[1])

#Call method
hits = wServer.doGoogleSearch(key, searchStr, 0, \
        10, False, "", False, "", "utf-8", "utf-8")

#Print results
print "\nResults\n============================="
print len(hits.resultElements), "Hits . . ."
for hit in hits.resultElements:
    print "\nURL:", hit.URL
    print "Title:", hit.title
    print "Desc:", hit.snippet
```

soap_wsdl.py

```
Available Methods
========================
[u'doGoogleSearch', u'doGetCachedPage',
 u'doSpellingSuggestion']

doGoogleSearch Args
====================
  key         string
  q           string
  start       int
  maxResults  int
  filter      boolean
  restrict    string
  safeSearch  boolean
  lr          string
  ie          string
  oe          string

Results
==============================
10 Hits . . .

URL: http://www.python.org/
Title: <b>Python</b> Language Website
Desc: Home page for <b>Python</b>, an interpreted,
interactive, object-oriented, extensible<br>
programming language. It provides an extraordinary
combination of clarity and <b>...</b>

URL: http://www.python.org/download/
Title: Download <b>Python</b> Software
Desc: The original implementation of <b>Python</b>,
written in C.

URL: http://www.python.org/doc/
Title: <b>Python</b> Documentation Index
Desc: Official tutorial and references, including
library/module usage, Macintosh<br> libraries,
language syntax, extending/embedding, and the
<b>Python</b>/C API.
. . .
```

Output of soap_wsdl.py

Index

How can we make this index more useful? Email us at indexes@samspublishing.com

How can we make this index more useful? Email us at indexes@samspublishing.com

How can we make this index more useful? Email us at indexes@samspublishing.com

U

X-Y

REGISTER THIS BOOK

Register this book and unlock benefits exclusive to the owners of this book.

Registration benefits can include

- Additional content
- Book errata
- Source code, example files, and other downloads
- Increased membership discounts
- Discount coupons
- A chance to sign up to receive content updates, information on new editions, and more

Book registration is free and takes only a few easy steps:

1. Go to **www.samspublishing.com/register**
2. Enter the book's ISBN (found above the barcode on the back of your book).
3. You will be prompted to either register for or log in to samspublishing.com.
4. Once you have completed your registration or log in, you will be taken to your "My Registered Books" page.
5. This page will list any benefits associated with each title you register, including links to content and coupon codes.

The benefits of book registration vary with each book, so be sure to register every Sams Publishing book you own to see what else you might unlock at **www.samspublishing.com/register**